I0009904

The Complete Guide to Building AI Agent Workflows with LangGraph and CrewAI

Robert J. Godwin

Copyright © 2025 by Robert J. Godwin

All rights reserved. No part of this publication may be reproduced, distributed, or transmitted in any form or by any means, including photocopying, recording, or other electronic or mechanical methods, without the prior written permission of the publisher, except in the case of brief quotations embodied in critical reviews and certain other non commercial uses permitted by copyright law.

Table of content

Table of content

Preface

The world of artificial intelligence is shifting—rapidly. Not long ago, building intelligent systems meant working with isolated models that could perform one task at a time. Today, we stand on the edge of a new paradigm: **autonomous, collaborative AI agents** that work together in structured workflows to complete complex, multi-step objectives.

This book is born out of both fascination and necessity. As a developer, I found myself inspired by the promise of tools like **LangGraph** and **CrewAI**—frameworks that bring structure, coordination, and memory to the otherwise fragmented world of agent-based applications. Yet, I also noticed a gap. While blog posts and demos offered glimpses into what's possible, there was no unified, step-by-step guide that could take you from beginner to builder, from tinkerer to architect.

That's where this book comes in.

"The Complete Guide to Building AI Agent Workflows with LangGraph and CrewAI" is more than just a technical manual—it's a roadmap for developers, entrepreneurs, and innovators who want to understand not just how these systems work, but why they matter. Whether you're building an autonomous research assistant, a business workflow automation tool, or a virtual team of decision-makers, this book will show you how to architect solutions that are **modular, scalable, and intelligent by design**.

You won't just learn how to write code—you'll learn how to think in systems. You'll explore the internal logic of multi-agent workflows, understand the differences between tools like LangGraph and CrewAI, and gain confidence in designing, deploying, and debugging real-world applications. Most importantly, you'll build. Through carefully structured chapters, hands-on examples, and real-world use cases, you'll apply what you learn immediately.

Along the way, I'll share personal insights—lessons learned from experimenting with early agent stacks, debugging frustrating edge cases, and watching autonomous agents take on increasingly complex roles with minimal human guidance. I hope these reflections help bridge the gap between concept and creation, between inspiration and implementation.

This book is for the curious, the builders, the forward-thinkers. If you're someone who believes in the power of automation, collaboration, and AI—not just as buzzwords, but as practical tools for transformation—then you're in the right place.

Let's build the future together—one agent at a ti

Introduction

What This Book Covers

Artificial Intelligence is no longer confined to isolated tasks like generating text or analyzing data. Today, we're building **autonomous agents**—systems that can reason, plan, and collaborate with each other to accomplish complex goals. The next leap in AI isn't just about making better models—it's about making **smarter systems**.

This book is a **comprehensive guide to building intelligent multi-agent workflows** using two of the most powerful and emerging tools in this space: **LangGraph** and **CrewAI**.

You'll learn how to:

- Design and implement **multi-agent architectures** using graph-based or crew-based paradigms.

- Structure workflows that allow agents to **communicate**, **delegate**, and **collaborate**.

- Integrate tools, memory, APIs, and logic to make agents **context-aware** and **autonomous**.

- Deploy your solutions to production environments with performance, scalability, and security in mind.

Whether you're building a research assistant, automating workflows, or creating a virtual team of AI specialists—this book will equip you with the tools and mental models needed to bring your ideas to life.

Why Multi-Agent Systems Matter

As AI becomes more capable, our expectations rise. A single prompt is no longer enough; we now want systems that can **manage tasks, respond dynamically, learn from context, and make decisions**—not unlike a team of professionals.

Multi-agent systems enable:

- **Decomposition of tasks** into specialized sub-processes.

- **Parallel execution**, speeding up operations.

- **Autonomy**, reducing human micromanagement.

- **Scalability**, as systems evolve and adapt to changing needs.

Frameworks like **LangGraph** provide the structure to define agent workflows as state machines or graphs, allowing you to control execution paths, loops, and decisions. On the other hand, **CrewAI** offers a more human-like collaboration model, where agents take on roles, coordinate tasks, and act as a team.

In short: these aren't just tools—they're stepping stones toward the future of intelligent automation.

Who This Book Is For

This book is written for:

- **Python developers** interested in AI and automation.

- **Machine learning engineers** exploring agent-based architectures.

- **Tech entrepreneurs** prototyping AI products or services.

- **AI enthusiasts and hobbyists are curious** about building smarter workflows.

You don't need a PhD in AI, but a solid understanding of Python and basic programming logic will help you get the most out of this book. If you've built apps with LangChain, worked with

OpenAI APIs, or used frameworks like FastAPI—you're more than ready.

How to Use This Book

This is a **practical, hands-on guide**, not a theoretical textbook. Each chapter builds on the last, starting from foundational concepts and moving toward fully functional systems. Here's how you can get the most from it:

- **Follow along with the code examples.** Every major concept is demonstrated with real code, so you can experiment as you read.

- **Use the projects as blueprints.** Adapt them to fit your own use cases or combine ideas from different chapters.

- **Refer back often.** Think of this book as both a guide and a reference—you can return to specific chapters as you build more advanced systems.

A companion GitHub repository is included, giving you access to all the sample code, configuration files, and resources referenced throughout the book.

Tools & Environment Setup

Before we dive in, let's make sure you're set up with the right tools. Throughout the book, we'll be using:

- **Python 3.10+**

- **LangGraph** – for building graph-based agent workflows

- **CrewAI** – for orchestrating agent collaboration

- **LangChain** – to provide core agent interfaces and tool integrations

- **OpenAI API** (or other LLM providers like Anthropic or Cohere)

- **Vector databases** like Chroma, Weaviate, or Pinecone (for agent memory)

- **FastAPI** or Flask (for deploying your agents as services)

We'll guide you step-by-step through installing and configuring each tool when it first appears in the book, so don't worry if some of these are unfamiliar right now.

By the end of this book, you won't just know *what* LangGraph and CrewAI are—you'll know **how to use them** to design intelligent, flexible, and production-ready agent workflows that reflect the future of AI.

Let's begin.

Would you like to move into **Chapter 1** next or create the GitHub repo outline first?

Chapter 1: Understanding AI Agents and Multi-Agent Systems

1.1 What Are AI Agents?

In the simplest terms, an **AI agent** is a software program that can make decisions and act on its own to achieve a goal.

Unlike traditional code that follows a fixed set of instructions, AI agents operate with **autonomy**—they evaluate situations, select actions, and learn from feedback. They don't just run code; they *think*, *reason*, and *adapt*.

Breaking It Down: Perception, Reasoning, and Action

To really understand what an AI agent is, it helps to think in terms of three core capabilities:

1. **Perceive** – The agent takes in inputs (like user prompts, documents, API data).

2. **Reason** – It interprets that input, applies logic (often powered by a language model), and decides what to do.

3. **Act** – It performs a task: answering, writing, querying a database, or calling a tool.

This loop can repeat across multiple steps as the agent works toward completing a task or solving a problem.

LLMs Supercharge Agents

What makes this current generation of AI agents so powerful is their integration with **large language models (LLMs)** like GPT-4 or Claude. These models give agents:

- **Natural language understanding** (so they can interact in plain English)

- **Reasoning capabilities** (like planning, summarizing, or debugging)

- **Flexibility** to handle a wide range of tasks with minimal training

Before LLMs, agents had to be programmed for very specific tasks. Now, a single LLM-backed agent can tackle anything from composing emails to writing code—if guided correctly.

Not Just Smart—Autonomous

Let's be clear: not every tool that uses AI is an agent.

An AI-powered search bar? Not really an agent.

But when you give the system a goal—*"Find top competitors for this startup and summarize their strengths"—*and it breaks that into subtasks, decides how to research, pulls in data, and returns a final report—that's an **agent at work**.

A Quick Analogy: The Helpful Assistant

Think of an AI agent like a highly capable virtual assistant.

You give it a job (e.g., "Plan my week"), and it doesn't just reply once—it thinks through what's required, checks your calendar, identifies conflicts, makes suggestions, and updates your schedule. It's not a one-off answer; it's **ongoing support with initiative**.

That's what sets agents apart: **they take initiative based on context** and can interact with their environment to get things done.

Key Components of Modern AI Agents

To function well, an agent typically includes:

- **A core LLM**: The brain that handles understanding and reasoning.

- **A set of tools**: APIs or functions it can call (e.g., search, code execution).

- **Memory**: So it can remember context over time.

- **A goal or task**: A specific objective to guide its decisions.

Some agents are simple—they answer questions. Others are complex—they build strategies, write code, analyze data, or coordinate with other agents.

Personal Insight: The First Time It "Clicked"

When I first built an agent with LangChain and gave it access to a calculator tool, I remember asking, *"What's 15% of 1378?"* The agent paused, "thought," and called the calculator tool by itself. That moment felt magical. I wasn't programming steps—I was giving goals, and the agent figured it out. That shift—from instructions to autonomy—is what makes agents so exciting.

1.2 Single vs Multi-Agent Architectures

When building intelligent systems, one of the first design decisions you'll face is whether to go with a **single-agent** or a **multi-agent** architecture. Both have their place—but the right choice depends on what you're trying to achieve.

Let's break it down.

What Is a Single-Agent Architecture?

A **single-agent system** is exactly what it sounds like: one agent, powered by an LLM or a logic engine, handles the entire task pipeline on its own. It receives an input, processes it, possibly calls tools, and delivers an output.

These systems are often:

- Simpler to build and debug

- Easier to deploy

- Ideal for straightforward or narrowly scoped tasks

Example use cases:

- A chatbot that answers questions

- A code generator based on prompts

- A document summarizer

You can think of single-agent systems like a solo freelancer—you give them a task, and they deliver the work end-to-end.

Where Single-Agent Systems Fall Short

While single-agent setups are great for fast prototyping, they often hit limitations as complexity grows. Here's why:

- **Cognitive overload:** Expecting one agent to plan, research, write, validate, and revise often leads to inefficiency and error.

- **Task switching:** The agent has to constantly context-switch, which isn't ideal for models with token or memory limits.

- **Harder to scale:** As you add more functionality, the single agent can become bloated with conditional logic and role ambiguity.

Personal insight: In early projects, I kept trying to force one agent to do it all—research, draft, fact-check, even deploy. Eventually, I realized I was building a fragile tower of prompts. Things started clicking when I split the work across specialized agents with clear responsibilities.

Enter Multi-Agent Architecture

In a **multi-agent system**, each agent has a clearly defined role. Instead of one agent doing everything, different agents focus on different stages or types of tasks—just like members of a team.

This division of labor has huge benefits:

- **Modularity** – You can update or improve one agent without affecting the rest.

- **Parallelization** – Agents can work simultaneously on different subtasks.

- **Specialization** – Each agent can be optimized for a specific goal (e.g., summarizing, validating, searching).

- **Robustness** – If one agent fails, others can pick up the slack or flag the issue.

Example use case:
Let's say you're building a financial research assistant. You might have:

- A *Planner Agent* to define subtasks

- A *Search Agent* to gather data from the web

- A *Summarizer Agent* to clean up findings

- A *Reviewer Agent* to ensure quality and accuracy

Together, they create a more intelligent, flexible, and scalable system than any one agent alone could deliver.

Communication Is Key

In multi-agent setups, communication between agents becomes the backbone of the system. This might involve passing messages, updating shared memory, or triggering state transitions.

Frameworks like **LangGraph** and **CrewAI** are designed to manage this interaction:

- LangGraph lets you define workflows as graphs with decision points, memory sharing, and custom flow control.

- CrewAI gives you a human-like team model, with agents operating as roles within a coordinated unit.

Each framework offers a different flavor of multi-agent architecture—but both help you **orchestrate collaboration** instead of juggling chaos.

When to Choose What

Criteria	Single Agent	Multi-Agent
Task complexity	Simple or linear	Complex, multi-stage, or open-ended
Speed to prototype	Fast	Moderate
Scalability	Limited	High
Maintenance	Gets harder as logic grows	Easier with modular roles

| Performance under load | Can bottleneck | Parallel execution is possible |
| Collaboration or delegation | Not suitable | Built-in support for team-like dynamics |

In Summary

- **Single-agent systems** are fast and lightweight—perfect for quick tools or narrowly focused apps.

- **Multi-agent architectures** shine when you're dealing with layered, dynamic, or long-running workflows.

Understanding the strengths and trade-offs of each approach is foundational for building effective AI systems. And as you'll see throughout this book, combining the **right agents with the right orchestration tools** unlocks a whole new level of intelligence and automation.

In the next section, we'll explore real-world examples of multi-agent workflows—and how they're quietly revolutionizing industries.

1.3 Real-World Applications of Multi-Agent Workflows

Multi-agent systems aren't just an academic concept or a flashy tech demo—they're powering real solutions across industries today. As workflows grow more complex, the need for intelligent, modular, and scalable automation becomes undeniable. Multi-agent architectures offer exactly that.

Let's explore where and how they're being used in the real world.

1. Business Process Automation

Businesses are drowning in repetitive, time-consuming tasks—report generation, market research, customer outreach, internal documentation. A single AI agent can handle some of it, but a team of specialized agents working together? That's where transformation begins.

Example:
An AI-driven sales assistant crew might include:

- A *Lead Researcher Agent* to identify and qualify potential leads.

- A *Proposal Generator Agent* to tailor outreach based on client needs.

- A *Follow-up Agent* to monitor responses and schedule meetings.

This kind of workflow mirrors what human teams do—but it's faster, cheaper, and scalable.

Insight: I've seen startups replace entire sales support teams using multi-agent systems with clear SOPs (Standard Operating Procedures) encoded into each agent. The structure was familiar; the speed was game-changing.

2. AI Content Creation & Publishing

Content generation has evolved beyond asking ChatGPT for an article. Multi-agent workflows allow for structured content pipelines, where each agent plays a specialized editorial role.

Example:

- *Planner Agent*: Outlines the content structure.

- *Writer Agent*: Drafts each section.

- *Editor Agent*: Refines tone, checks grammar, and optimizes for SEO.

- *Fact-Checker Agent*: Validates accuracy using external tools.

You're not just generating content—you're building a miniature newsroom, run entirely by autonomous agents.

3. Software Development & Debugging

Coding copilots are useful, but a multi-agent development crew is a whole different level. Instead of relying on one assistant to write everything, you distribute tasks across agents trained for each phase.

Example:

- *Requirements Agent*: Breaks down the user story into dev tasks.

- *Coder Agent*: Writes the initial implementation.

- *Tester Agent*: Writes and runs tests.

- *Refactor Agent*: Optimizes and cleans up code.

This system can even detect bugs or inefficiencies and loop back tasks automatically—creating a continuous delivery pipeline powered by AI.

4. Research and Knowledge Synthesis

In domains like legal, scientific, or financial research, multi-agent systems are making sense of massive, unstructured data. Instead of dumping everything on one agent, tasks are decomposed and handled in parallel.

Example:
For market analysis:

- *Data Collector Agent* scrapes websites and APIs.

- *Summarizer Agent* condenses findings by category.

- *Insight Agent* identifies patterns and anomalies.

- *Report Generator Agent* creates a polished executive summary.

What once took teams of analysts days or weeks can now happen in hours—or less.

5. Customer Support Systems

Modern support teams juggle tickets, FAQs, knowledge bases, and live chats. Multi-agent systems can replicate that workflow:

Example:

- *Triage Agent* identifies the issue type.

- *Solution Agent* searches internal docs and drafts a response.

- *Escalation Agent* routes unresolved cases to a human or logs them for later review.

These systems can also **learn** from past resolutions, becoming more accurate and efficient over time.

6. Personal Productivity Systems

Think of this as a personalized AI team for your life or work.

Example:

- *Calendar Agent* schedules and optimizes meetings.

- *Email Agent* drafts responses based on intent.

- *Focus Agent* blocks distractions and recommends priorities.

- *Task Agent* breaks down goals into daily to-dos.

This isn't futuristic—it's happening now, thanks to LangGraph, CrewAI, and frameworks that allow multiple agents to share memory and coordinate intelligently.

7. Simulations and Training Environments

Game developers, behavioral researchers, and corporate trainers use multi-agent systems to simulate complex environments with interacting entities.

Example:

- In a negotiation simulation, each agent plays a stakeholder with specific goals, constraints, and personalities.

- The system evolves based on decisions, mimicking real-world dynamics.

This has massive potential in HR, education, and even AI safety research

Why It Works

The success of these applications comes down to five key strengths of multi-agent workflows:

- **Scalability** – Handle large, varied workloads without overloading a single agent.

- **Specialization** – Assign the right agent to the right task.

- **Parallelism** – Speed up complex workflows by running agents simultaneously.

- **Modularity** – Debug, improve, or replace parts of the system independently.

- **Resilience** – If one agent fails or stalls, others can adapt or take over.

In Summary

Multi-agent workflows aren't just a theoretical improvement over single-agent systems—they're enabling practical, high-value automation across industries. From sales and content to software and strategy, they offer a structured, scalable way to turn AI into a true workforce.

As we dive deeper into LangGraph and CrewAI in upcoming chapters, you'll see how to design, deploy, and optimize these systems yourself—starting with the basics, and building up to powerful, real-world applications.

1.4 The LLM Revolution and Autonomous Agents

The rise of Large Language Models (LLMs) like GPT-4, Claude, and Gemini has radically changed what's possible in artificial intelligence. We're no longer talking about basic bots that follow rigid rules. We're talking about powerful systems that understand context, generate human-like language, and reason through complex tasks. This leap has directly fueled the evolution of autonomous agents.

What Changed with LLMs

Before LLMs, most AI systems were narrow in focus. They required structured data, rigid pipelines, and explicit instructions.

They could handle classification tasks, automate form processing, or maybe predict outcomes—but only within strict boundaries.

Then LLMs arrived, and suddenly we had models that could:

- Understand open-ended questions

- Generate context-aware, nuanced text

- Chain reasoning across multiple steps

- Interact using natural language, not code

This opened the door to agents that didn't just *execute commands*, but could *think through* problems.

Why LLMs Are the Foundation of Modern Agents

At the heart of every smart AI agent today is an LLM. It acts as the brain—interpreting goals, breaking down tasks, deciding what to do next, and even evaluating its own outputs. Here's why they work so well in this role:

- **Contextual Understanding:** LLMs track long conversations and draw logical conclusions from scattered inputs.

- **Versatile Reasoning:** They can perform math, write code, explain concepts, or solve logic puzzles—without task-specific training.

- **Language-Native Interface:** Since they "speak" natural language, they can interact with humans, tools, or even other agents seamlessly.

This flexibility is why LLMs are not just a backend component—they're the interface *and* the engine of autonomous systems.

From Language Models to Autonomous Agents

An LLM on its own is impressive, but still passive. Ask it a question, and it answers. That's it. What makes it autonomous is when we wrap it in a decision-making loop with memory, tools, and goals. That's how we go from a smart assistant to a true agent.

Autonomous agents powered by LLMs typically include:

- A *planner* that breaks down tasks or goals

- *Tool integration* (e.g., search, API calls, databases)

- *Memory* to remember past decisions or knowledge

- *State management* to track what's done and what's next

Combine those elements, and the LLM doesn't just respond—it acts.

LLMs and Multi-Agent Collaboration

One of the most powerful shifts brought by LLMs is their ability to coordinate across multiple agents. Since each agent can speak in natural language and interpret goals, they can collaborate just like human teammates—sharing tasks, negotiating decisions, or passing information down a pipeline.

This is where frameworks like LangGraph and CrewAI shine. They turn LLMs into structured agent teams, each with a role, a memory, and a shared objective. Instead of scaling vertically (one smarter model), we scale horizontally (many focused agents working in sync).

Real Impact, Real Fast

Just a few years ago, it would've taken months to build a multi-agent system with hand-coded logic and rules. Today, thanks to LLMs and modern frameworks, developers can build robust, semi-autonomous systems in days. We're seeing:

- Customer support teams running on AI

- Research assistants that synthesize literature

- AI CEOs coordinating entire agent-led startups

Personal Insight: I've built prototypes where agents handled everything from scraping data to writing reports and pitching ideas—working together with almost zero human input beyond the initial goal. It was like running a remote team, except everyone was AI.

The Bottom Line

LLMs didn't just improve AI—they reshaped it. They gave rise to agents that can plan, reason, communicate, and act with surprising autonomy. And as these models continue to evolve, we're just scratching the surface of what agent-based systems can do.

In the next section, we'll break down the core building blocks of these systems—concepts like tasks, memory, state, and collaboration—that will help you design your own intelligent agent workflows.

1.5 Key Concepts: Tasks, Tools, Memory, State, Collaboration

To build effective multi-agent systems, you need to understand the foundational concepts that bring autonomy and intelligence to life. These five pillars—**Tasks, Tools, Memory, State**, and **Collaboration**—are the building blocks of every agent workflow. Mastering them will give you the power to design agents that aren't just reactive but capable of planning, executing, and adapting.

Let's break each one down.

1. Tasks: The Unit of Work

At the core of every agent lies a *task*. Tasks define what needs to be done—whether it's answering a question, generating content, querying a database, or coordinating with another agent.

A well-defined task is:

- **Goal-oriented**: It has a clear purpose.

- **Context-aware**: It can use past inputs or ongoing conversations.

- **Decomposable**: If it's too complex, the agent can break it down into subtasks.

Tip: Think of tasks like a to-do list. If you hand an agent a messy list with vague goals, you'll get vague results. Clarity matters.

2. Tools: Extending the Agent's Abilities

LLMs are great at language, but they're not all-knowing. Tools bridge that gap. Tools are external capabilities—APIs, databases, calculators, web scrapers, file readers—that an agent can call to perform specialized actions.

Popular examples include:

- **Search tools** for looking up real-time data

- **Math functions** for complex calculations

- **APIs** to pull in or send data to other systems

- **Code execution environments** for dynamic programming

When you give agents tools, you move beyond conversation and into action. They can make decisions *and* execute them.

Insight: In one workflow I built, an agent used tools to fetch financial news, summarize key insights, and then generate a market update email—all in one loop. Tools turned a smart responder into a full assistant.

3. Memory: Knowing What Came Before

Memory allows an agent to remember past interactions, facts, or steps it has taken. Without memory, every decision is made in a vacuum—causing redundancy, inefficiency, and confusion.

Types of memory include:

- **Short-term memory**: Temporary context from the current session

- **Long-term memory**: Persistent knowledge across tasks or sessions

- **Tool-specific memory**: Saving data outputs for use in later steps

Memory enables continuity. An agent can refer to previous answers, improve over time, or learn user preferences.

Example: A writing agent that remembers the tone, style, and structure from previous articles produces more consistent and on-brand content.

4. State: Tracking Progress and Logic

State is how the system keeps track of what's happening right now. It's like a status dashboard for the agent's mind. It holds:

- What step the agent is on

- What's already been completed

- What information has been collected

- What the agent is waiting on next

State ensures that workflows don't lose their place or repeat steps unnecessarily. It's especially important in multi-step or multi-agent workflows where agents need to pass data between stages.

Analogy: Imagine baking a cake. Without tracking the state, you might forget whether you added sugar—or add it twice. State keeps things organized and accurate.

5. Collaboration: Working with Other Agents

This is where things get exciting. Agents don't need to work alone. In a multi-agent system, each agent can specialize, share context, and coordinate efforts toward a shared goal.

Collaboration requires:

- **Defined roles**: Each agent knows its function (e.g., researcher, writer, reviewer)

- **Shared memory/state**: Agents can access each other's outputs

- **Communication protocols**: Agents speak a shared language, often through natural-language messages

Example: In a content production system, one agent researches a topic, another drafts the article, and a third agent edits it. Each one picks up where the other left off—just like a human team.

Personal Insight: I've seen teams create "agent hierarchies," where a lead agent delegates subtasks to junior agents and aggregates their results. It mirrors real-world org structures and scales surprisingly well.

Putting It All Together

When tasks are defined clearly, tools are integrated smartly, memory is used effectively, state is tracked consistently, and collaboration is well-orchestrated—your agents become capable, coordinated, and autonomous. These concepts aren't just theoretical—they're what separate basic chatbots from robust, intelligent systems.

In the chapters ahead, we'll take these concepts and put them into practice using LangGraph and CrewAI. You'll see exactly how to structure agent workflows around these pillars and watch simple components evolve into powerful systems.

Chapter 2: The Multi-Agent Tech Stack

In the previous chapter, we laid the foundation by exploring the core concepts behind AI agents and multi-agent systems. Now, it's time to turn theory into practice by examining the technology stack that powers modern agent workflows. This chapter will guide you through the essential components: the frameworks that orchestrate agents, the APIs that fuel them, the tools that extend their functionality, and the memory systems that give them continuity.

Whether you're building a lightweight assistant or a full-blown autonomous team, understanding this ecosystem is the first step toward making the right architectural decisions.

2.1 Overview of LangGraph, CrewAI, and AgentVerse

Multi-agent systems are no longer theoretical—they're powering real-world automation, research, and business applications. Thanks to open-source frameworks like **LangGraph**, **CrewAI**, and **AgentVerse**, you don't need to build everything from scratch.

Each of these platforms brings a unique approach to managing and coordinating AI agents. In this section, we'll explore how they work, what they're best suited for, and walk through actual code examples to help you get started.

LangGraph: Build Agent Workflows as Graphs

LangGraph is built on top of LangChain and allows you to define agents and their workflows as **stateful graphs**. Think of nodes as agents or tasks, and edges as transitions based on logic or conditions.

Key Features

- Graph-based workflows with state tracking

- Supports loops, conditional branches

- Compatible with all LangChain tools (tools, chains, memory)

When to Use

- Complex workflows requiring branching or step-by-step logic

- Coordination between agents where sequence matters

Installation

pip install langgraph langchain openai

Basic Example: A Two-Agent Chat Flow

This example shows how two agents (a **Researcher** and a **Writer**) collaborate to answer a query.

```python
from langgraph.graph import StateGraph, END

from langchain.chat_models import ChatOpenAI

from langchain.tools import tool

from langchain.agents import AgentExecutor, create_tool_calling_agent


# Step 1: Define tools

@tool

def search_tool(query: str) -> str:
```

```python
    return f"Fetched info about {query}"


# Step 2: Define agents

llm = ChatOpenAI(model="gpt-3.5-turbo", temperature=0)


researcher_tools = [search_tool]

researcher = create_tool_calling_agent(llm,
tools=researcher_tools)

researcher_executor = AgentExecutor(agent=researcher,
tools=researcher_tools)


writer_tools = []

writer = create_tool_calling_agent(llm, tools=writer_tools)

writer_executor = AgentExecutor(agent=writer,
tools=writer_tools)


# Step 3: Define graph
```

```python
workflow = StateGraph()


workflow.add_node("research", researcher_executor)

workflow.add_node("write", writer_executor)


workflow.set_entry_point("research")

workflow.add_edge("research", "write")

workflow.add_edge("write", END)


graph_executor = workflow.compile()


# Step 4: Run

input_data = {"input": "Write an article about Mars
colonization"}

result = graph_executor.invoke(input_data)
```

```
print(result)
```

This structure is great for defining explicit flows. Each node handles a specific step, and the state passes cleanly between agents.

CrewAI: Agents as a Team with Roles

CrewAI is inspired by real-world teams. Instead of defining a workflow graph, you define **roles** (like CEO, Researcher, Developer), and assign tasks to each agent. The framework handles delegation and sequencing.

Key Features

- Role-based team structure

- Natural language coordination

- Simple and fast to deploy

When to Use

- Projects with clearly defined roles (e.g., content creation, marketing analysis)

- When rapid prototyping or business-focused outcomes are needed

Installation

pip install

Basic Example: Researcher + Writer Crew

```
from  import Agent, Task, Crew

from langchain.chat_models import ChatOpenAI


llm = ChatOpenAI(temperature=0, model="gpt-4")


# Step 1: Define Agents
researcher = Agent(

   role="Researcher",

   goal="Gather in-depth data on space travel",

   backstory="Expert in space science and astronomy",
```

```python
    llm=llm

)


writer = Agent(

    role="Writer",

    goal="Craft compelling blog posts using researched data",

    backstory="Experienced tech writer and communicator",

    llm=llm

)


# Step 2: Define Tasks
task1 = Task(

    description="Find key facts about Mars colonization",

    agent=researcher

)
```

```python
task2 = Task(

    description="Write a 500-word blog post based on the
research",

    agent=writer,

    depends_on=[task1]

)


# Step 3: Create Crew

crew = Crew(

    agents=[researcher, writer],

    tasks=[task1, task2],

    verbose=True

)


crew.kickoff()
```

This approach mirrors how human teams work, making it perfect for business and content workflows.

AgentVerse: Simulation and Strategy-Focused Agents

AgentVerse is a sandbox for experimenting with **agent-to-agent communication**, strategy, and environment simulation. It's great for research, prototyping, or exploring complex decision logic.

Key Features

- Simulated environments

- Agent strategy and policy definitions

- Customizable message protocols

When to Use

- Simulating cooperative or competitive agent behavior

- Experimenting with emergent behaviors or message protocols

Installation

```
pip install agent verse
```

Basic Example: Chat Simulation Between Agents

```
from agent verse.environments import DialogueEnvironment

from agent verse.agents import Agent


env = DialogueEnvironment()


agent_a = Agent(name="Negotiator A", strategy="aggressive")

agent_b = Agent(name="Negotiator B", strategy="defensive")


env.add_agent(agent_a)

env.add_agent(agent_b)


env.run(num_turns=5)
```

Unlike LangGraph or CrewAI, AgentVerse is more experimental. It's suited for simulations where outcomes are uncertain and agents must negotiate or adapt.

Summary

Feature	LangGraph	CrewAI	AgentVerse
Model	Graph-based workflows	Role-based team orchestration	Simulation & strategy
Complexity	Medium	Low	Medium to High
Best For	Automation pipelines	Business processes	Research and simulation

Control Flow	Explicit graph transitions	Natural delegation	Simulated turns/policies
Setup Time	Moderate	Quick	Moderate

Final Thoughts

LangGraph, CrewAI, and AgentVerse are each excellent tools—but they shine in different use cases. If you need logic-heavy pipelines, go with LangGraph. For productivity apps, CrewAI's simplicity wins. And if you're testing agent communication strategies, AgentVerse gives you the simulation flexibility.

2.2 Comparing Frameworks: Strengths and Use Cases

Choosing the right multi-agent framework often comes down to your project's goals, complexity, and the level of control you need over agent behavior. LangGraph, CrewAI, and AgentVerse all offer distinct strengths, and understanding their differences helps you build more effective and maintainable systems. Let's break down their core design philosophies, ideal use cases, and provide example scenarios that illustrate where each framework excels.

LangGraph: Designed for Structured Workflows

LangGraph treats your workflow like a flowchart. Each node represents a function, a decision point, or an agent. It's ideal when your system needs predictable execution paths, clear transitions, or when debugging requires explicit visibility into agent steps.

Strengths

- Fine-grained control over execution

- Easy to visualize logic and state transitions

- Excellent for pipeline-based agent orchestration

- Tight integration with LangChain tools and memory systems

Best Use Cases

- Knowledge retrieval followed by reasoning and content generation

- Task-oriented pipelines with clear sequencing and branching

- Systems needing long-term memory and custom state tracking

Scenario: Automating Technical Blog Writing with a Review Loop

A blog writing workflow includes three steps: research, draft writing, and review. LangGraph allows you to loop back to research if the reviewer finds missing details.

```
from langgraph.graph import StateGraph, END

from langchain.agents import create_tool_calling_agent,
AgentExecutor

from langchain.chat_models import ChatOpenAI


llm = ChatOpenAI(model="gpt-4", temperature=0)


# Define agents

researcher_executor = AgentExecutor(
```

```python
    agent=create_tool_calling_agent(llm, tools=[]),

    tools=[]

)

writer_executor = AgentExecutor(

    agent=create_tool_calling_agent(llm, tools=[]),

    tools=[]

)

reviewer_executor = AgentExecutor(

    agent=create_tool_calling_agent(llm, tools=[]),

    tools=[]

)


# Build workflow

workflow = StateGraph()

workflow.add_node("research", researcher_executor)

workflow.add_node("write", writer_executor)
```

```
workflow.add_node("review", reviewer_executor)


workflow.set_entry_point("research")

workflow.add_edge("research", "write")

workflow.add_edge("write", "review")

workflow.add_conditional_edges("review", lambda state:
"research" if state["needs_more_info"] else END)


graph = workflow.compile()

graph.invoke({"input": "How does LangGraph handle
memory?"})
```

LangGraph's conditional edge makes it easy to re-route tasks
based on internal state—perfect for iterative processes.

CrewAI: Simplicity and Role-Based Thinking

CrewAI is built for fast iteration and productivity. You define
agents with roles and goals, give them tasks, and the system figures

out the coordination. It's less about control flow and more about high-level delegation.

Strengths

- Extremely easy to set up

- Intuitive agent design using goals and backstories

- Built-in task dependencies

- Great for solo developers and startup teams

Best Use Cases

- Content teams, marketing agents, business research crews

- Non-linear workflows that don't need rigid sequencing

- Scenarios where natural language task management makes sense

Scenario: Marketing Strategy Crew

A business wants a team of AI agents to create a new product launch plan. The roles include Researcher, Analyst, and Strategist.

```python
from  import Agent, Task, Crew

from langchain.chat_models import ChatOpenAI


llm = ChatOpenAI(model="gpt-4")


researcher = Agent(

    role="Researcher",

    goal="Identify competitors and market trends",

    backstory="Expert in market research",

    llm=llm

)


analyst = Agent(

    role="Analyst",
```

```python
    goal="Evaluate product strengths and pricing models",

    backstory="Data-driven analyst focused on SaaS businesses",

    llm=llm
)


strategist = Agent(

    role="Strategist",

    goal="Craft a compelling launch strategy",

    backstory="Senior product strategist with startup experience",

    llm=llm
)


task1 = Task(description="Find competitors for our new AI productivity app", agent=researcher)

task2 = Task(description="Analyze competitor pricing models", agent=analyst, depends_on=[task1])
```

```
task3 = Task(description="Develop a go-to-market strategy based
on research and analysis", agent=strategist, depends_on=[task1,
task2])


crew = Crew(agents=[researcher, analyst, strategist], tasks=[task1,
task2, task3], verbose=True)

crew.kickoff()
```

With just a few lines, you have a coordinated team executing tasks
with interdependencies, each agent using its role context to guide
behavior.

AgentVerse: Experimental Simulations and Dialogue Control

AgentVerse offers a more customizable, simulation-first approach.
It's not designed around workflows or roles but around
environments, strategies, and inter-agent dialogue. You define
how agents interact, compete, or cooperate over time.

Strengths

- Excellent for testing strategies, behaviors, and communication styles

- Powerful environment simulation support

- Ideal for research, games, and negotiation experiments

Best Use Cases

- AI game development (e.g., NPC interactions)

- Research simulations (e.g., negotiation, swarm behavior)

- Agent policy comparison and benchmarking

Scenario: Two Bots Negotiating a Deal

```
from agent verse.environments import DialogueEnvironment

from agent verse.agents import Agent


env = DialogueEnvironment()
```

```
agent1 = Agent(name="Alice", strategy="compromise")

agent2 = Agent(name="Bob", strategy="competitive")


env.add_agent(agent1)

env.add_agent(agent2)


env.run(num_turns=5)
```

You can tweak the strategies and see how negotiation plays out. AgentVerse is less prescriptive, giving you flexibility to define behavior models.

Quick Decision Matrix

Feature	LangGraph	CrewAI	AgentVerse
Control Flow	High	Medium	Custom / Simulated

Setup Complexity	Moderate	Low	Moderate
Workflow Modeling	Graph-based	Role-based	Dialogue / Policy-based
Ideal Users	Engineers, DevOps	Creators, Entrepreneurs	Researchers, Game Devs
Reusability	High	Medium	Low–Medium

Final Take

LangGraph gives you architectural clarity. CrewAI gives you speed and simplicity. AgentVerse gives you creative freedom. Pick LangGraph when you want to design complex flows with branching logic. Choose CrewAI when time-to-deploy matters and you want results fast. Use AgentVerse when you're exploring behavior, experimenting with simulations, or building something unconventional.

Next, we'll dive into how to integrate LLM providers like OpenAI, Anthropic, and Hugging Face into these frameworks effectively.

2.3 LLM APIs: OpenAI, Anthropic, Hugging Face

Large Language Models (LLMs) are the engines powering intelligent agents. While LangGraph, CrewAI, and AgentVerse help orchestrate how agents behave and interact, the real "thinking" comes from the models they rely on. Choosing the right LLM API—OpenAI, Anthropic, or Hugging Face—can influence not only the capabilities of your system but also its cost, latency, and compliance with data regulations.

Let's break down the core strengths of each platform and explore how to integrate them into a multi-agent system with clean, working examples.

OpenAI: The Gold Standard for Versatile, High-Performance Models

OpenAI's GPT-4 and GPT-3.5 models are widely adopted due to their strong general reasoning, code generation, and structured output capabilities. The API is fast, well-documented, and deeply integrated with popular agent frameworks.

Key Highlights

- GPT-4 excels at reasoning-heavy tasks and role-based dialogues

- System messages allow fine-tuning of agent persona

- Supports function calling for tool-based agents

- Offers powerful embedding models (text-embedding-3-small, text-embedding-3-large)

Integration Example: GPT-4 with LangChain AgentExecutor

```
from langchain.chat_models import ChatOpenAI

from langchain.agents import create_tool_calling_agent,
AgentExecutor

from langchain.tools import Tool


# Setup OpenAI agent
```

```python
llm = ChatOpenAI(model="gpt-4", temperature=0)


tools = [

  Tool.from_function(

    name="Calculator",

    func=lambda x: str(eval(x)),

    description="Evaluates simple math expressions."

  )

]


agent = create_tool_calling_agent(, tools)

executor = AgentExecutor(agent=agent, tools=tools)


response = executor.invoke({"input": "What is 12 * (7 + 3)?"})

print(response["output"])
```

The function calling interface makes it easy for GPT-4 to decide when to call external tools, allowing agents to be more autonomous in handling tasks.

Anthropic: Safer, Dialogue-Optimized Interactions

Anthropic's Claude models are known for their alignment with human intent, extended context windows (up to 200K tokens), and gentle instruction following. Claude tends to avoid hallucination more than GPT-4, especially when fine-tuned with proper prompts.

Key Highlights

- Excellent at extended, multi-turn conversations

- Ideal for summarization, customer support, and analysis tasks

- Native support for JSON mode and minimal formatting hallucination

Integration Example: Claude with CrewAI via Custom LLM Wrapper

While CrewAI doesn't support Anthropic out-of-the-box, it works seamlessly if wrapped using LangChain's ChatAnthropic.

```python
from  import Agent, Task, Crew

from langchain.chat_models import ChatAnthropic


llm = ChatAnthropic(model="clause-3-opus-20240229",
temperature=0)


agent = Agent(

    role="Compliance Analyst",

    goal="Summarize regulatory documents and flag risks",

    backstory="Specialist in financial regulations",

    llm=llm

)


task = Task(description="Review the document and highlight risk
sections", agent=agent)

crew = Crew(agents=[agent], tasks=[task], verbose=True)

crew.kickoff()
```

Claude's strong summarization ability makes it a great fit for enterprise use cases involving lengthy content.

Hugging Face: Flexibility, Control, and On-Prem Deployments

Hugging Face offers a wide variety of open-source and hosted LLMs like Mistral, Mixtral, LLaMA, Falcon, and more. While not always as strong as proprietary models in out-of-the-box performance, they provide unmatched flexibility and privacy.

Key Highlights

- Supports private deployment via transformers and text-generation-inference

- Great for compliance-sensitive environments (on-prem or VPC setups)

- Wide range of models for fine-tuning and customization

- Integration with Hugging Face Hub and Spaces

Integration Example: Hosted Mistral Model with LangChain

```python
from long chain.lmms import HuggingFaceEndpoint


llm = HuggingFaceEndpoint(


endpoint_url="https://api-inference.huggingface.co/models/mist
ralai/Mistral-7B-Instruct-v0.2",

  huggingfacehub_api_token="YOUR_API_TOKEN",

  temperature=0.5

)


response = llm.invoke("What are some use cases of multi-agent AI
systems?")

print(response)
```

You can also self-host LLMs using the text-generation-webui or
vLLM, giving you complete control over latency, cost, and
customization.

Quick Comparison Table

Feature	OpenAI	Anthropic	Hugging Face
Top Models	GPT-4, GPT-3.5	Claude 3 Opus, Sonnet	Mistral, LLaMA, Falcon
Max Context Window	128K (GPT-4-Turbo)	200K (Claude 3)	Depends on model/version
Function Calling	Native	JSON structured outputs	Manual via custom logic
Fine-tuning Options	Limited	Not available	Wide range of models

Ideal Use Cases	General-purpose agents	Safe, long-form dialogue	Private or open-source AI
Deployment	Cloud only	Cloud only	Cloud + Local

Which API Should You Choose?

- **Go with OpenAI** if you want plug-and-play power, function calling, and top-tier performance with minimal setup.

- **Choose Anthropic** for projects needing safer, more human-aligned outputs or ultra-long context conversations.

- **Pick Hugging Face** when you need local control, compliance, or want to experiment with open models and fine-tuning.

Ultimately, you can even combine them across different agents within the same workflow. For example, use GPT-4 for reasoning, Claude for summarization, and Mistral for fast classification. That flexibility is one of the biggest advantages of modern multi-agent systems.

2.4 Integrating Tools and APIs

One of the core strengths of multi-agent systems is their ability to interact with external tools and APIs. This is where agents evolve from passive responders to proactive problem-solvers. Integrating tools allows your agents to retrieve real-time data, perform calculations, query databases, and even control software workflows—essentially bridging the gap between language and action.

Let's break down the concept, why it matters, and how to do it properly using LangGraph and CrewAI.

Why Tool Integration Matters

LLMs are powerful, but they're not omniscient. They can't access your calendar, make API calls, or browse a private database without external tools. That's where **tool use** comes in. A well-designed agent system equips agents with tools and defines when and how to use them intelligently.

Examples:

- Use a weather API to fetch live temperature data

- Run a Python function to solve a math problem

- Query a vector database to retrieve memory

- Hit a company CRM API to summarize customer records

Tool Integration with LangGraph

LangGraph supports tool usage via agents powered by LangChain's AgentExecutor or function-calling wrappers. Here's how you can set it up:

Step 1: Define the Tools

```python
from langchain.tools import Tool

import requests


def get_weather(location: str) -> str:

    response = requests.get(f"http://wttr.in/{location}?format=3")

    return response.text
```

```python
weather_tool = Tool(

    name="WeatherTool",

    func=get_weather,

    description="Get current weather for a given city."

)
```

Step 2: Setup the Agent with Tools

```python
from langchain.chat_models import ChatOpenAI

from langchain.agents import create_tool_calling_agent,
AgentExecutor


llm = ChatOpenAI(model="gpt-4", temperature=0)

agent = create_tool_calling_agent(llm, [weather_tool])

executor = AgentExecutor(agent=agent, tools=[weather_tool])
```

```
executor.invoke({"input": "What's the weather like in Tokyo
today?"})
```

The agent now knows how and when to use the tool in response
to a user query. This abstraction keeps the system dynamic and
easily extensible.

Tool Integration with CrewAI

CrewAI structures tools differently but achieves similar results.
Each agent can be equipped with a set of tools that enhance its
ability to complete tasks.

Step 1: Define Your Tool Function

```
def stock_price_checker(company: str) -> str:

    response =
requests.get(f"https://api.example.com/stock/{company}")

    return f"{company} stock is currently trading at
{response.json()['price']}"
```

Step 2: Create a Custom Tool Class

```
from crewai_tools import BaseTool
```

```python
class StockPriceTool(BaseTool):

    name = "Stock Price Checker"

    description = "Fetches the current stock price for a given
company."


    def _run(self, company: str):

        return stock_price_checker(company)
```

Step 3: Attach Tool to CrewAI Agent

```python
from import Agent


stock_tool = StockPriceTool()

finance_agent = Agent(

    role="Financial Analyst",

    goal="Provide up-to-date stock market insights",
```

```
    backstory="Specialist in financial markets and equity analysis",

    tools=[stock_tool]

)
```

With this setup, the agent is now able to make real API calls as part of its decision-making process.

Use Case Example: Integrating Multiple Tools

Let's look at a more complex example. You want an agent that:

- Searches Google for a company

- Fetches stock prices

- Summarizes sentiment from recent news articles

You can build a toolkit with three functions:

1. Web search (SerpAPI)

2. Stock API lookup

3. News summarization (using LLM)

Then attach all of them to the agent and allow it to dynamically choose which tool to use depending on the user request. This is the foundation of **agentic reasoning with tool orchestration**.

Best Practices for Tool Integration

- **Always sanitize input**: Especially when integrating user data with APIs

- **Document tool usage** clearly so the agent knows when and how to invoke them

- **Use descriptions** to guide LLMs in choosing the right tool

- **Rate-limit and retry** API calls to avoid failures

- **Log tool usage** to understand agent decisions and improve future iterations

Summary

Tools and APIs are not just optional add-ons—they are essential enablers of intelligent behavior. Whether you're using

LangGraph's structured approach or CrewAI's team-based framework, effective tool integration is what makes agents truly useful.

Once you grasp how to integrate tools, you unlock the ability to create agents that do more than talk—they act. Next, we'll explore how to persist knowledge and long-term memory in your agents using vector databases and memory systems like Pinecone, Chroma, and Weaviate.

2.5 Vector Stores and Memory Systems (Pinecone, Chroma, Weaviate)

LLMs are excellent at language understanding, but they don't have memory in the way traditional software does. If you want your AI agents to recall past interactions, reference documents, or build long-term context, you'll need an external memory system. That's where vector stores come in.

Vector stores like **Pinecone**, **Chroma**, and **Weaviate** allow you to persist knowledge as embeddings—mathematical representations of text—so agents can search, retrieve, and reference data across sessions.

Why Vector Stores Matter in Agent Workflows

Imagine you're building a customer service agent that can:

- Recall previous tickets

- Retrieve knowledge base articles

- Store custom user preferences

An LLM alone can't do that. You need memory—specifically **retrieval-augmented generation (RAG)**. A vector store acts as an intelligent memory layer where agents can:

- Store facts or documents as embeddings

- Search semantically (not just by keyword)

- Get the most relevant content for context

This keeps responses accurate, contextual, and personalized.

Example Workflow: Embedding, Storing, and Retrieving

Let's walk through the standard pattern:

1. Convert text into embeddings

2. Store the embeddings in a vector database

3. At runtime, embed a query and retrieve the most similar stored chunks

Pinecone: Scalable, Production-Ready Vector Store

Step 1: Install and Setup Pinecone

```
pip install pinecone-client openai
```

```
import pinecone

from openai.embeddings_utils import get_embedding


pinecone.init(api_key="YOUR_API_KEY",
environment="gcp-starter")

index = pinecone.Index("langgraph-memory")


# Convert and upsert data
```

```python
text = "LangGraph enables complex agent workflows with ease."

vector = get_embedding(text, engine="text-embedding-3-small")

index.upsert([("doc1", vector)])
```

Step 2: Retrieve Memory at Query Time

```python
query = get_embedding("How to build agent workflows?")

results = index.query(query, top_k=3, include_metadata=True)

print(results)
```

Pinecone is reliable, fast, and scalable—ideal for production deployments.

Chroma: Lightweight, Local-First Vector Store

Chroma is an open-source alternative that runs locally or in your own environment. Perfect for small-scale apps, prototyping, or users who want more control.

Step 1: Install and Initialize

```
pip install chromadb
```

```python
import chromadb

from langchain.embeddings.openai import OpenAIEmbeddings


chroma_client = chromeadb.Client()

collection = chroma_client.create_collection("agent_knowledge")


# Add documents
collection.add(

    documents=["LangGraph is great for multi-agent workflows."],

    metadatas=[{"source": "doc1"}],

    ids=["id1"]

)
```

Step 2: Query Similar Content

```python
results = collection.query(
```

```
    query_texts=["How can I build AI agents?"],

    n_results=2

)

print(results)
```

Chroma is great for personal projects and educational use, and it integrates easily with LangChain.

Weaviate: Semantic Search and Hybrid Filters

Weaviate offers a mix of structured filters, semantic search, and hybrid querying—all useful in multi-agent systems that rely on both logic and learning.

Step 1: Setup with LangChain

```
pip install weaviate-client
```

```
import weaviate

client = weaviate.Client("http://localhost:8080")
```

```python
# Add a simple schema for documents

client.schema.create_class({

    "class": "AgentDocs",

    "vectorizer": "text2vec-openai",

    "properties": [{"name": "content", "dataType": ["text"]}]

})


# Add a document

client.data_object.create(

    data_object={"content": "CrewAI helps you manage multiple
agents."},

    class_name="AgentDocs"

)
```

Step 2: Query for Memory

```python
response = client.query.get("AgentDocs",
["content"]).with_near_text({
```

```
    "concepts": ["multi-agent systems"]

}).with_limit(2).do()



print(response)
```

Weaviate is ideal for hybrid search, where you want to combine semantic similarity with structured metadata (e.g., filtering by user or task).

Which Vector Store Should You Use?

Feature	Pinecone	Chroma	Weaviate
Hosting	Cloud	Local or self-hosted	Local + Cloud options
Scalability	High	Medium	Medium–High

Open Source	No	Yes	Yes
Filtering Support	Basic metadata	Metadata + simple filters	Hybrid filters + metadata
Best For	Production AI apps	Local testing/dev	Complex, hybrid search

Best Practices for Using Memory

- **Chunk large documents**: Break down large text into manageable parts for better retrieval

- **Store metadata**: Include tags like source, timestamp, or category

- **Embed consistently**: Use the same embedding model for storage and query

- **Limit retrieval scope**: Only retrieve the top relevant items (top_k=3–5 is typical)

- **Re-rank if needed**: Consider re-ranking retrieved items with LLMs for higher accuracy

Summary

Without memory, your agents are goldfish—powerful but forgetful. Vector stores like Pinecone, Chroma, and Weaviate unlock persistent knowledge, giving your agents the ability to think with context, recall with precision, and interact with users meaningfully.

In the next chapter, we'll begin architecting your first real multi-agent workflow using LangGraph or CrewAI—where memory, tools, and reasoning come together in a functional system.

Chapter 3: Getting Started with LangGraph

LangGraph is quickly emerging as one of the most effective tools for building multi-agent workflows. Inspired by the concept of computation graphs and enhanced for the specific needs of agent orchestration, LangGraph brings structure, modularity, and clarity to complex systems. This chapter will walk you through getting started with LangGraph—from setup to building your first simple yet functional workflow.

We'll also look at LangGraph's core concepts like states, edges, and cycles, and how they map directly to intelligent agent behaviors. By the end of this chapter, you'll be confident in creating your first LangGraph flow and understanding how to maintain and scale it.

3.1 Installing and Configuring LangGraph

Getting started with LangGraph is straightforward if you have a basic Python environment set up. This section walks you through everything you need—from installing dependencies to verifying that LangGraph is correctly configured for building multi-agent workflows.

Before diving in, let's clarify one thing: LangGraph is built on top of LangChain and is designed to manage agent behavior through stateful, graph-based execution. If you're already familiar with LangChain or working with language models, you'll find LangGraph a natural progression.

Step 1: Set Up Your Environment

It's best to isolate your development environment to avoid dependency conflicts. Create a virtual environment using venv:

python -m venv langgraph-env

Activate the environment:

On macOS/Linux:

 source langgraph-env/bin/activate

On Windows:

.\langgraph-env\Scripts\activate

Keeping your environment isolated like this ensures your LangGraph experiments won't interfere with other projects.

Step 2: Install Required Packages

LangGraph works alongside LangChain and an LLM provider like OpenAI or Anthropic. Here's the minimal set of packages you'll need:

pip install langgraph langchain openai

If you plan to use Anthropic, you can install their package too:

pip install anthropic

For visualizing graphs or debugging workflows, tools like networkx or graphviz might also come in handy:

pip install networkx matplotlib

At this point, your environment is set up to start using LangGraph.

Step 3: Configure Your LLM API Key

LangGraph itself doesn't tie you to one LLM provider. It integrates easily with whichever one you prefer. For OpenAI, set your API key like this:

```
export OPENAI_API_KEY="your-openai-api-key"  #
macOS/Linux

set OPENAI_API_KEY="your-openai-api-key"    # Windows
```

If you're using Anthropic or others, follow the same pattern, adjusting the environment variable as needed (e.g., ANTHROPIC_API_KEY).

I recommend storing these keys in a .env file if you're working with many different services. You can load them using the dotenv package:

```
pip install python-dotenv
```

Then, at the top of your Python scripts:

```
from dotenv import load_dotenv

load_dotenv()
```

This keeps your credentials secure and your code clean.

Step 4: Test Your Setup with a Simple Graph

Let's build a basic LangGraph that takes user input and summarizes it using OpenAI's GPT model.

```python
from langgraph.graph import StateGraph, END

from langchain.chat_models import ChatOpenAI


# Step 1: Define the summarizer node

def summarize_node(state):

    llm = ChatOpenAI(temperature=0)

    response = llm.predict(f"Summarize the following text: {state['input']}")

    state['summary'] = response

    return state


# Step 2: Initialize the graph

builder = StateGraph()

builder.add_node("summarizer", summarize_node)

builder.set_entry_point("summarizer")
```

```
builder.set_finish_point(END)


# Step 3: Compile and run

graph = builder.compile()

input_state = {"input": "LangGraph helps you build AI
workflows using graphs."}

output = graph.invoke(input_state)


print("Summary:", output["summary"])
```

This confirms your setup is working correctly. The node
summarize_node handles the interaction with the LLM, and
LangGraph orchestrates the workflow using the defined state and
graph topology.

Pro Tip: Version Control Dependencies

Use pip freeze > requirements.txt to save your environment, and
consider tools like poetry or pip-tools if your project grows.

Final Notes

Installing and configuring LangGraph is just the beginning. What makes it powerful is how it scales: you can start with a single node and gradually introduce complex logic, state transitions, and feedback loops.

3.2 LangGraph Architecture: States, Edges, Nodes, Cycles

To build robust and flexible AI workflows, you need a structure that's easy to reason about, modular enough to adapt as needs evolve, and powerful enough to handle complex coordination logic. LangGraph delivers this by modeling agent flows as graphs—with **states**, **nodes**, **edges**, and **cycles** forming the core components. This architecture not only simplifies orchestration but makes workflows transparent and debuggable.

Let's explore each part of the architecture and then walk through a practical implementation that ties them together.

States: The Shared Memory

In LangGraph, the **state** is a Python dictionary that holds all the data passed between nodes. It functions as the shared memory of the system, and every node has access to it.

Think of the state as a live notebook where inputs, outputs, decisions, and other variables are continuously updated. You can initialize it like this:

```
state = {

    "user_input": "How can LangGraph help structure multi-agent
    workflows?"

}
```

As nodes process the input, they add or modify keys in this dictionary.

Nodes: The Processing Units

A **node** in LangGraph is simply a Python function (or any callable) that takes the state as input, does some work, and returns the updated state.

Here's a simple node that generates a summary using OpenAI:

```
from langchain.chat_models import ChatOpenAI


def summarize_node(state):

    llm = ChatOpenAI(temperature=0)

    response = llm.predict(f"Summarize: {state['user_input']}")

    state["summary"] = response
```

```
    return state
```

Nodes are modular—you can use them in different graphs, compose them into larger structures, and debug them independently.

Edges: Connecting the Flow

Edges define the order of execution. They tell LangGraph which node to run next after a particular node completes. This is where LangGraph shines over linear pipelines—because you can define conditional logic, branching, and even feedback loops.

```
builder.add_edge("summarizer", "evaluator")
```

You can also define conditional transitions using functions:

```
def route_by_quality(state):

    return "reviser" if state["quality_score"] < 0.8 else "END"


builder.add_conditional_edges("evaluator", route_by_quality)
```

Cycles: Iteration and Feedback

Cycles are one of the most powerful features of LangGraph. They allow you to loop over certain nodes, enabling behaviors like reflection, critique, retries, and refinement—essential for autonomous agents.

A classic use case is a Review-Revise loop:

```
builder.add_edge("reviewer", "reviser")

builder.add_edge("reviser", "reviewer")  # cycle
```

You can control how many times a loop runs using state variables like a counter, or add a feedback node that determines when to break the loop

Full Example: Multi-Stage Summary Workflow

Let's build a complete graph that includes all core components:

```
from langgraph.graph import StateGraph, END

from langchain.chat_models import ChatOpenAI


def summarize_node(state):
```

```python
    llm = ChatOpenAI(temperature=0)

    summary = llm.predict(f"Summarize: {state['user_input']}")

    state["summary"] = summary

    return state


def critique_node(state):

    llm = ChatOpenAI(temperature=0)

    critique = llm.predict(f"Critique this summary:
{state['summary']}")

    state["critique"] = critique

    return state


def revise_node(state):

    llm = ChatOpenAI(temperature=0)

    revised = llm.predict(f"Revise this summary based on critique:
{state['summary']}\nCritique: {state['critique']}")

    state["revised_summary"] = revised
```

```python
    return state


def check_quality(state):

    return "revise" if "needs improvement" in
state["critique"].lower() else END



# Build the graph

builder = StateGraph()

builder.add_node("summarize", summarize_node)

builder.add_node("critique", critique_node)

builder.add_node("revise", revise_node)


builder.set_entry_point("summarize")

builder.add_edge("summarize", "critique")

builder.add_conditional_edges("critique", check_quality, {

    "revise": "revise",
```

```
    END: END

})

builder.add_edge("revise", "critique")  # cycle


graph = builder.compile()


output = graph.invoke({"user_input": "LangGraph provides a
way to structure AI agent workflows."})

print("Final Output:", output.get("revised_summary",
output.get("summary")))
```

This example captures an iterative summary improvement
process: generate → critique → revise → re-critique → exit when
satisfied.

Why This Architecture Matters

The flexibility of LangGraph's architecture makes it suitable for
building anything from simple pipelines to sophisticated agent
teams. You can:

- Visualize logic clearly

- Debug workflows step-by-step

- Reuse and compose agent components

- Introduce feedback, retries, and conditional behavior easily

From experience, working with such an architecture helps reduce the cognitive load of managing many moving parts. You stop thinking in terms of linear code and start thinking in terms of intelligent flow.

Next, we'll dive into building your first real-world workflow with LangGraph, and how to apply everything we've covered so far to create something tangible and useful.

3.3 Building a Simple Workflow with LangGraph

Now that you understand the architectural building blocks of LangGraph—states, nodes, edges, and cycles—it's time to put them to work. In this section, we'll build a simple, functioning multi-agent workflow that simulates a task you might encounter in a real-world AI application: summarizing a document and then classifying its tone.

This hands-on example introduces the core mechanics of LangGraph, while keeping things easy to follow and extensible. Once you're comfortable here, scaling up to more complex graphs will feel natural.

Use Case: Summarize and Classify

Our goal is to:

1. Accept user input (e.g., an article or paragraph)

2. Generate a concise summary

3. Classify the tone of the summary as positive, neutral, or negative

To accomplish this, we'll use LangChain's ChatOpenAI model, plug it into a LangGraph structure, and define the flow step-by-step.

Step 1: Set Up the Environment

Make sure you have the required packages installed:

pip install langchain openai langgraph

Then, set your OpenAI API key as an environment variable:

export OPENAI_API_KEY=your_openai_api_key

Step 2: Define the State

The shared state is a dictionary that stores the user's input, the summary, and the classification. Here's what it might look like at runtime:

```
{

    "user_input": "LangGraph is a new framework that helps structure agent workflows...",

    "summary": "LangGraph simplifies the structuring of agent workflows.",

    "tone": "Neutral"

}
```

Step 3: Create the Nodes

Each node is a function that performs a specific task and updates the state.

Summarizer Node

```python
from langchain.chat_models import ChatOpenAI



def summarize_node(state):

    llm = ChatOpenAI(temperature=0)

    response = llm.predict(f"Summarize
this:\n\n{state['user_input']}")

    state["summary"] = response

    return state
```

Tone Classifier Node

```python
def classify_tone_node(state):

    llm = ChatOpenAI(temperature=0)

    prompt = (
```

```
      f"Classify the tone of the following summary as Positive,
Neutral, or Negative:\n\n"

      f"{state['summary']}"

  )

  tone = llm.predict(prompt).strip()

  state["tone"] = tone

  return state
```

Step 4: Build the Graph

With the nodes in place, define the graph using StateGraph:

```
from langgraph.graph import StateGraph, END


builder = StateGraph()


builder.add_node("summarize", summarize_node)

builder.add_node("classify_tone", classify_tone_node)
```

```
builder.set_entry_point("summarize")

builder.add_edge("summarize", "classify_tone")

builder.add_edge("classify_tone", END)


graph = builder.compile()
```

Step 5: Run the Workflow

You can now run the graph by passing in the initial state.

```
initial_state = {

    "user_input": "LangGraph allows developers to create modular,
repeatable agent workflows by defining nodes and edges in a
stateful graph."

}


result = graph.invoke(initial_state)
```

```
print("Summary:", result["summary"])

print("Tone:", result["tone"])
```

You should see something like:

Summary: LangGraph enables modular, repeatable agent workflows using a stateful graph structure.

Tone: Neutral

Why This Workflow Matters

This workflow captures the essence of LangGraph: breaking down tasks into composable, traceable units. Each node serves a clear purpose, and the state ensures information is shared cleanly between steps.

From personal experience, starting with small workflows like this makes it easier to grow into more complex systems. You might later insert a node that evaluates the summary's quality, adds retries, or routes different tones to different agents. The graph model makes those additions intuitive.

3.4 Debugging and Visualizing Agent Flows

As your LangGraph workflows evolve from simple chains to intricate graphs with branching logic and feedback loops, understanding how data flows and where things might go wrong becomes essential. Debugging and visualization aren't just for troubleshooting—they also help you design smarter, more efficient agent systems.

LangGraph makes it relatively straightforward to inspect, trace, and visualize your workflows. In this section, we'll cover techniques for:

- Logging internal state

- Inspecting transitions

- Visualizing the graph structure

- Handling unexpected errors

These tools will give you confidence in your implementation and insight into how your agents are actually behaving.

Step 1: Logging State Transitions

The easiest way to understand what's happening inside your graph is to log the state at key points. You can log directly inside your node functions:

```
def summarize_node(state):

    print("Running summarizer with input:", state["user_input"])

    llm = ChatOpenAI(temperature=0)

    response = llm.predict(f"Summarize
this:\n\n{state['user_input']}")

    state["summary"] = response

    print("Generated summary:", response)

    return state
```

Logging like this provides transparency, especially when working with unpredictable LLM outputs. You can also log inputs, outputs, or intermediate steps to a file or external logging service (e.g., Loguru, Sentry) in production.

Step 2: Using Custom Callbacks

LangGraph supports callbacks that can hook into the lifecycle of node execution. This lets you centralize logging or tracing without modifying the node code directly.

Here's a simple callback example:

```python
from langgraph.graph import Callback
```

```python
class PrintCallback(Callback):

    def on_node_start(self, node_name, state):

        print(f"Starting node: {node_name}")


    def on_node_end(self, node_name, state):

        print(f"Finished node: {node_name}")
```

Then pass the callback to your graph:

```python
graph = builder.compile()

result = graph.invoke(initial_state, callbacks=[PrintCallback()])
```

This approach scales better as your graph grows.

Step 3: Visualizing the Graph

LangGraph includes built-in support for graph visualization via graphviz. You can export your graph structure as a diagram for documentation or debugging.

Install the package:

pip install graphviz

Then export and render your graph:

import graphviz

dot = builder.get_graphviz()

dot.render("workflow_diagram", format="png", view=True)

This generates a PNG of your node structure, showing entry points, transitions, and terminal nodes. It's especially helpful when designing loops, forks, or conditional edges.

Step 4: Catching and Handling Errors

Errors in one node can propagate through the system if not handled properly. You can wrap risky logic in try/except blocks to prevent crashes and provide fallback behavior.

```python
def classify_tone_node(state):

    try:

        llm = ChatOpenAI(temperature=0)

        prompt = f"Classify this text: {state['summary']}"

        tone = llm.predict(prompt).strip()

        state["tone"] = tone

    except Exception as e:

        print("Error in tone classifier:", str(e))

        state["tone"] = "Unknown"

    return state
```

In larger systems, it's also common to implement custom error-handling nodes or define error paths in the graph.

Step 5: Inspecting Final Output

After the graph finishes running, inspecting the final state gives you a complete snapshot of all transformations:

```python
result = graph.invoke(initial_state)

for key, value in result.items():

    print(f"{key}: {value}")
```

This lets you verify that each part of the flow worked as expected—and is especially useful when developing or writing test cases.

Personal Insight

Debugging agent workflows is a lot like debugging real-world teams. You're not just checking code; you're tracing how information flows, how decisions are made, and whether the agents understood the task. Adding visibility into your workflow early on saves hours of head-scratching later.

I've found that even simple logs or visualizations often expose subtle logic issues, like a node receiving unexpected input, or a cycle that never terminates. Think of debugging and visualization as your agent's user interface—it might not be customer-facing, but it's essential for developer sanity.

What's Next

Now that you've learned how to build and debug LangGraph workflows, let's explore how to make your graphs reusable, modular, and scalable. The next section covers best practices for creating composable graph components that reduce duplication and improve maintainability.

3.5 Reusability and Modularity in LangGraph

As LangGraph workflows grow in complexity, maintaining clean, reusable, and modular code becomes essential. Rather than building one massive monolithic graph, the smart approach is to design workflows as composable blocks—each responsible for a specific task. This makes your agent systems easier to debug, test, maintain, and extend.

LangGraph encourages this modular mindset through reusable node functions, subgraphs, and graph templates. In this guide, we'll walk through practical patterns for achieving modularity, demonstrate how to encapsulate logic, and show how to reuse components across multiple workflows.

Reusable Node Functions

Each node in a LangGraph graph is just a Python function that receives and returns a shared state dictionary. Keeping your node functions single-purpose and stateless makes them reusable across different graphs. Here's a simple reusable node:

```python
def summarize_text(state):

    input_text = state["input"]

    llm = ChatOpenAI(temperature=0)

    state["summary"] = llm.predict(f"Summarize:\n{input_text}")

    return state
```

This summarizer can be reused in various workflows—customer support, news aggregation, internal reports—simply by feeding it different input data through the shared state.

Creating Graph Templates

Sometimes you need to reuse not just a node but a whole sequence of steps. LangGraph allows you to define graph templates that act like subroutines.

```python
from langgraph.graph import StateGraph
```

```python
def build_summarization_graph():

    builder = StateGraph()

    builder.add_node("summarize", summarize_text)

    builder.set_entry_point("summarize")

    builder.set_finish_point("summarize")

    return builder.compile()
```

Now you can plug this subgraph into a larger workflow as a component, without rewriting logic or state handling. This also makes testing easier since subgraphs can be invoked independently.

Using Edge Labels for Reusability

Edge labels in LangGraph help control flow by enabling conditional branching. You can use them to generalize behavior in reusable graphs. For instance, a "review" node can return labels like "pass" or "fail", and downstream logic can change based on those outcomes.

```python
def review_summary(state):
```

```
if "excellent" in state["summary"]:

    return "pass"

return "fail"
```

This kind of modular decision-making supports dynamic workflows while keeping the logic contained and clean.

Composing Graphs Together

LangGraph doesn't require you to do everything in one place. You can construct separate graphs for input parsing, classification, generation, or summarization, and then stitch them together.

```
input_graph = build_input_parser()

processing_graph = build_summarization_graph()

postprocess_graph = build_tone_analyzer()


main_graph = StateGraph()

main_graph.include_graph(input_graph)

main_graph.include_graph(processing_graph)
```

```
main_graph.include_graph(postprocess_graph)
```

This keeps your architecture clean, avoids duplication, and allows independent updates to each module.

Real-World Benefit: Maintainability

In my own work, breaking down complex agent pipelines into modular subgraphs has been a lifesaver. When a component (like a summarizer or a memory writer) needs an upgrade, I can update it in one place and watch the improvements ripple across every workflow that uses it. This kind of modular structure also makes onboarding collaborators easier—they can understand and improve parts without needing to digest the entire graph at once.

Testability and Mocking

Reusable functions and graphs are easier to test. Since each node operates independently on a shared state, you can write unit tests for nodes in isolation:

```
def test_summarize_text():

    dummy_state = {"input": "LangGraph helps build agent workflows."}

    result = summarize_text(dummy_state)
```

```
assert "summary" in result
```

You can also mock LLMs during testing to avoid token costs or rate limits.

Tips for Modularity

- Keep node functions short and focused

- Store business logic in external utilities when possible

- Use consistent state keys and naming across graphs

- Favor small, single-responsibility graphs and compose them

- Document inputs and outputs clearly

Conclusion

Reusability and modularity aren't optional—they're foundational if you want your agent workflows to scale cleanly and evolve over time. LangGraph gives you the flexibility to think in terms of small, interchangeable components. As your projects grow, this mindset will pay off in speed, clarity, and agility.

Chapter 4: Designing Complex LangGraph Workflows

As you gain fluency in LangGraph, you'll find yourself wanting more than simple sequential flows. Real-world systems demand dynamic routing, parallel processing, iterative improvement, memory sharing, and intelligent collaboration between agents. This chapter introduces you to designing advanced workflows in LangGraph—systems that can think, adapt, and evolve.

You'll learn to model decisions, handle feedback loops, coordinate agent behaviors, and debug complex flows. We'll also walk through a full case study that applies everything you've learned so far in a realistic scenario.

4.1 Dynamic Routing and Conditional Branching

Dynamic routing is one of the most powerful features in LangGraph. It allows your workflow to change course based on runtime conditions, agent outputs, or the state of the task. This flexibility enables intelligent decision-making within multi-agent systems, making your workflow adaptable rather than rigid.

Whether you're routing a user query to different expert agents or deciding between retrying a task or terminating it, conditional branching gives you granular control over your agent flow.

Why Dynamic Routing Matters

In traditional single-agent pipelines, workflows often follow a fixed path—step A to B to C. But real-world problems are rarely linear. Users might ask different types of questions, data might be incomplete, or a task might fail and need retrying. Dynamic routing handles all of these elegantly.

LangGraph allows you to define decision points using custom logic. You write a function that examines the current state and returns the next node to transition to. This allows your system to react contextually.

Building a Router Node

Let's walk through a simple example: a content generation workflow that can route requests based on the user's intent. The workflow will decide whether to summarize, translate, or analyze text.

Step 1: Define Your Router Function

```
def route_by_intent(state):

    intent = state.get("intent", "")

    if "summary" in intent.lower():

        return "summarizer"
```

```
    elif "translate" in intent.lower():

        return "translator"

    elif "analyze" in intent.lower():

        return "analyzer"

    return "default_handler"
```

This router function inspects the intent field from the shared state and returns the appropriate node name.

Step 2: Add the Nodes and Router to the Graph

```
from langgraph.graph import StateGraph


workflow = StateGraph()


# Add processing nodes

workflow.add_node("summarizer", summarize_text)

workflow.add_node("translator", translate_text)
```

```python
workflow.add_node("analyzer", analyze_text)

workflow.add_node("default_handler", handle_unknown_intent)


# Add the router node with dynamic edges

workflow.add_conditional_edges(

    "router",

    route_by_intent,

    {

        "summarizer": "summarizer",

        "translator": "translator",

        "analyzer": "analyzer",

        "default_handler": "default_handler"

    }

)


workflow.set_entry_point("router")
```

```
workflow.set_finish_point("default_handler")

graph = workflow.compile()
```

This structure gives you a flexible router node that can dispatch input to the appropriate processing agent based on the intent.

Making Routing More Context-Aware

You can go beyond simple keyword matching. For instance, you could combine semantic search, prompt engineering, or a lightweight classifier to predict intent.

Example using an LLM to detect intent:

```
def classify_intent_with_llm(state):

    user_input = state.get("input", "")

    response = openai.ChatCompletion.create(

        model="gpt-4",

        messages=[

            {"role": "system", "content": "Classify the user's intent as
one of: summarize, translate, analyze."},
```

```python
        {"role": "user", "content": user_input}

    ]

)

    label =
response["choices"][0]["message"]["content"].strip().lower()

    return label if label in ["summarize", "translate", "analyze"] else
"default_handler"
```

This allows dynamic routing based on the understanding of natural language rather than brittle rules.

Advanced Branching: Fallbacks and Error Handling

You can add more resilience by including fallback branches. For example:

```python
def route_with_fallback(state):

    try:

        # Complex routing logic here

        ...
```

```
    except Exception:

        return "error_handler"
```

And then in the graph:

```
workflow.add_node("error_handler", handle_error)

workflow.add_conditional_edges("router", route_with_fallback, {

    ...

    "error_handler": "error_handler"

})
```

Now, if routing fails, the system gracefully hands off control to an error handler instead of crashing.

Real-World Use Case

Imagine a customer support assistant that routes inquiries to a billing bot, technical assistant, or a general responder:

```
def support_router(state):
```

```
topic = detect_topic(state["message"])

return {

    "billing": "billing_bot",

    "tech": "tech_bot",

    "other": "generic_bot"

}.get(topic, "generic_bot")
```

This gives you a multi-intent support system with specialized agents that handle context-relevant tasks.

Tips for Designing Good Routing Logic

- **Keep logic explicit**: Avoid overly opaque ML models in routing unless needed.

- **Fallbacks are essential**: Always include a default or error path.

- **Test each route**: Simulate state transitions for every expected route.

- **Log routing decisions**: It helps with debugging and improving intent classification.

Conclusion

Dynamic routing and conditional branching transform LangGraph from a basic flow engine into a decision-aware system. Whether you're building chatbots, research agents, or process automation, the ability to direct flow based on live context unlocks new layers of intelligence and flexibility.

Start simple, then evolve your routers as your workflows mature. A well-designed router can reduce agent overload, increase modularity, and enhance overall system robustness.

4.2 Looping, Parallel Execution, and Feedback Loops

LangGraph offers robust support for advanced control flows such as loops, parallel execution, and feedback loops. These patterns are essential when building sophisticated multi-agent workflows that need to handle iteration, concurrent tasks, or result-based refinement.

Understanding how to implement these patterns allows you to create agents that not only perform tasks but also learn, adapt, and self-correct—key traits for building intelligent systems.

Looping in LangGraph

Loops are useful when an agent needs to retry a task, improve its output iteratively, or perform a sequence repeatedly based on certain conditions. You can implement loops by connecting nodes in a cycle and controlling the loop exit through state conditions.

Let's say you want an agent to generate a summary, get feedback, and improve it until it meets quality standards.

```python
def summarizer_node(state):

    # Generate summary

    summary = generate_summary(state["content"])

    return {"summary": summary, "feedback_count":
state.get("feedback_count", 0)}


def feedback_node(state):

    feedback = evaluate_summary(state["summary"])

    if feedback["score"] >= 0.8:

        return {"finished": True}
```

```
    return {"feedback_count": state["feedback_count"] + 1,
"finished": False}
```

Now connect the nodes in a loop:

```
graph = StateGraph()

graph.add_node("summarizer", summarizer_node)

graph.add_node("feedback", feedback_node)


def feedback_router(state):

    return "exit" if state.get("finished") else "summarizer"


graph.add_conditional_edges("feedback", feedback_router, {

    "summarizer": "summarizer",

    "exit": "__end__"

})
```

```
graph.set_entry_point("summarizer")

graph.add_edge("summarizer", "feedback")
```

The workflow will cycle through summarizer and feedback until the score threshold is met.

Parallel Execution

LangGraph allows you to run nodes concurrently using tool_node or parallel dispatch inside a node. This is extremely helpful when you want to query multiple sources, evaluate several options, or distribute work across agents.

Suppose you're building a research assistant that gathers information from different APIs:

```
def fetch_from_sources(state):

    from concurrent.futures import ThreadPoolExecutor


    def get_data(api):

        return call_api(api, state["query"])
```

```python
apis = ["api1", "api2", "api3"]

with ThreadPoolExecutor() as executor:

    results = list(executor.map(get_data, apis))

return {"results": results}
```

This function uses Python's threading to fetch data in parallel, reducing latency and increasing throughput.

You can also break this logic into separate LangGraph nodes if needed, especially when each agent performs distinct roles.

Feedback Loops

Feedback loops are useful for refining outputs based on reviews, test results, or human-in-the-loop feedback. This can be similar to a loop, but with a stronger emphasis on analysis and correction.

Here's an example workflow for code generation and review:

1. **Generator Agent**: Writes initial code

2. **Reviewer Agent**: Reviews for bugs or style issues

3. **Fixer Agent**: Updates code based on feedback

Each round produces better results through feedback and adjustment.

```
def review_code(state):

    feedback = code_review_tool(state["code"])

    state["feedback"] = feedback

    state["approved"] = feedback["score"] > 0.9

    return state


def route_review(state):

    return "__end__" if state["approved"] else "fixer"
```

Design Tips

- Use conditional_edges to break or continue loops based on feedback

- Use shared state keys (like approved, score, or iteration_count) to track progress

- Avoid infinite loops by capping iterations or using timeout checks

- Modularize each phase (e.g., generate, review, revise) to keep logic clean

Common Use Cases

- **Research and Summarization**: Gather multiple inputs, summarize iteratively, improve through feedback

- **Creative Generation**: Write → critique → rewrite cycles for stories, code, or copywriting

- **Decision Support**: Evaluate multiple options in parallel, then loop through refinement based on criteria

4.3 Agent Collaboration and Memory Sharing

Effective multi-agent workflows depend heavily on seamless collaboration and smart memory management. Just like in a human team, agents need to share knowledge, build context together, and pass the right data at the right time. Without that, they're just isolated bots. LangGraph makes agent collaboration and memory sharing intuitive by leveraging shared state and modular memory systems.

Why Agent Collaboration Matters

Agent collaboration is not just about passing data—it's about enabling coordinated decision-making. One agent might gather information, another might analyze it, and a third might act on it. Collaboration allows these roles to flow as part of a coherent strategy rather than separate silos.

For example, in a content generation pipeline:

- Agent A conducts research

- Agent B writes a draft based on the research

- Agent C edits and fact-checks the draft

Without collaboration and memory sharing, each of these agents would have to start from scratch.

Shared State in LangGraph

LangGraph manages memory through a shared state dictionary that gets passed and updated through each node in the graph.

This state acts as a collaborative whiteboard that all agents can read from and write to.

Here's how to initialize and use a shared state:

```
initial_state = {

    "topic": "AI agents",

    "research_notes": [],

    "draft": "",

    "final_output": ""

}
```

Each node can read or update this state.

Example: a Research Agent adds to research_notes:

```
def research_agent(state):

    notes = perform_web_research(state["topic"])

    state["research_notes"].append(notes)

    return state
```

Then, a Writing Agent can use those notes to generate a draft:

```python
def writing_agent(state):

    draft = generate_draft_from_notes(state["research_notes"])

    state["draft"] = draft

    return state
```

This pattern ensures every agent builds upon the work of the previous one.

Memory Sharing Strategies

While the shared state works well for small- to midsize workflows, complex applications may need persistent memory across sessions or large-scale knowledge access. That's where vector stores and memory systems come into play.

Let's integrate Pinecone for long-term memory:

```python
from long chain.vector stores import Pinecone

from langchain.embeddings.openai import OpenAIEmbeddings
```

```python
memory = Pinecone(index_name="agent-memory",
embedding_function=OpenAIEmbeddings())


def store_in_memory(state):

    memory.add_texts([state["draft"]], metadatas=[{"agent":
"writer"}])

    return state


def retrieve_memory(state):

    results = memory.similarity_search(state["topic"])

    state["memory_snippets"] = [r.page_content for r in results]

    return state
```

Now any agent can store or recall relevant context, even from past workflows.

Example: A Collaborative Multi-Agent Setup

Let's wire it all together in a LangGraph flow:

```
graph = StateGraph()
```

```
graph.add_node("research", research_agent)
```

```
graph.add_node("write", writing_agent)
```

```
graph.add_node("review", review_agent)
```

```
graph.add_node("store", store_in_memory)
```

```
graph.set_entry_point("research")
```

```
graph.add_edge("research", "write")
```

```
graph.add_edge("write", "review")
```

```
graph.add_edge("review", "store")
```

```
graph.add_edge("store", "__end__")
```

This pipeline enables clear collaboration: each agent picks up where the last left off, and the output is saved for future reuse.

Collaboration Pitfalls to Avoid

- **Overwriting State**: Be careful not to replace shared state blindly—always update it incrementally

- **Name Clashes**: Use clear, unique keys in the state dictionary to avoid conflicts

- **Tight Coupling**: Design agents to rely on specific state fields but not hardcoded behavior from other agents. This ensures modularity.

4.4 Case Study: Automated Research & Summarization Pipeline

Let's walk through a practical case study that showcases how LangGraph can be used to build a multi-agent workflow for research and summarization. This example demonstrates how agents can collaborate to extract insights from the web and generate concise summaries—something useful in journalism, marketing, academic reviews, and more.

Project Overview

We'll build a LangGraph workflow with three core agents:

1. **Research Agent** – Performs web search and gathers relevant content.

2. **Extraction Agent** – Extracts key information and facts.

3. **Summarization Agent** – Generates a concise, human-readable summary.

We'll also add a final **Storage Agent** to save the output and optionally push it to a database or file.

Step 1: Set Up Your Environment

Make sure the required libraries are installed:

pip install langgraph langchain openai duckduckgo-search

Set your OpenAI key:

import os

os.environ["OPENAI_API_KEY"] = "your-openai-key"

Step 2: Define Shared State

This shared dictionary will hold all inputs and outputs between agents:

```
initial_state = {

    "query": "Latest breakthroughs in quantum computing",

    "raw_results": [],

    "facts": [],

    "summary": ""

}
```

Step 3: Implement Agents

Research Agent

Uses DuckDuckGo to perform a basic search and return the top results.

```
from duckduckgo_search import DDGS


def research_agent(state):
```

```python
query = state["query"]

with DDGS() as ddgs:

    results = [r["body"] for r in ddgs.text(query, max_results=5)]

state["raw_results"] = results

return state
```

Extraction Agent

Extracts factual sentences using an LLM.

```python
from langchain.chat_models import ChatOpenAI


llm = ChatOpenAI(model="gpt-3.5-turbo")


def extraction_agent(state):

    combined_text = "\n".join(state["raw_results"])

    prompt = f"Extract key facts from the following content:\n\n{combined_text}"
```

```
response = llm.predict(prompt)

state["facts"] = response.split("\n")

return state
```

Summarization Agent

Generates a readable summary from the extracted facts.

```
def summarization_agent(state):

    facts = "\n".join(state["facts"])

    prompt = f"Summarize the following facts into a clear, concise
paragraph:\n\n{facts}"

    response = llm.predict(prompt)

    state["summary"] = response

    return state
```

Storage Agent (Optional)

Prints the final summary or stores it to a file.

```python
def storage_agent(state):

    with open("summary_output.txt", "w") as f:

        f.write(state["summary"])

    print("Summary saved to summary_output.txt")

    return state
```

Step 4: Build the LangGraph Workflow

```python
from langgraph.graph import StateGraph


graph = StateGraph()


graph.add_node("research", research_agent)

graph.add_node("extract", extraction_agent)

graph.add_node("summarize", summarization_agent)

graph.add_node("store", storage_agent)
```

```
graph.set_entry_point("research")

graph.add_edge("research", "extract")

graph.add_edge("extract", "summarize")

graph.add_edge("summarize", "store")

graph.add_edge("store", "__end__")


app = graph.compile()
```

Run the workflow:

```
output = app.invoke(initial_state)

print(output["summary"])
```

Outcome

This multi-agent system takes a research topic and autonomously delivers a clean, summarized overview. All steps—search, extraction, summarization, and output—are handled by modular agents that could be reused or upgraded independently.

Why This Matters

- **Scalable Automation**: You can run this pipeline repeatedly for different topics with minimal changes.

- **Reusable Logic**: Each agent can be plugged into other workflows.

- **Foundation for Complexity**: Add agents for citation generation, bias detection, or even cross-referencing with databases.

4.5 Troubleshooting LangGraph Issues

LangGraph is a powerful tool, but like any framework, it's not immune to bugs, misconfigurations, or user error. Whether you're building simple flows or complex agent interactions, knowing how to identify and fix issues is essential for scaling and maintaining your workflows. This section offers practical guidance for solving common problems and preventing future ones.

Common Error Types and Their Causes

1. **Graph Misconfigurations**
   Misconfigured nodes or edges are frequent culprits. This includes incorrect state transitions, missing edges, or

circular references without proper loop conditions.

Example:

Incorrect edge setup

graph.add_edge("node_a", "node_b") # but node_b is not defined

Solution: Double-check that all nodes referenced in add_edge() are registered with the graph before connecting them.

2. **State Mismatches**
    State mismatches happen when a node expects input data in a certain format or type and receives something else.

Example:

def process_node(state):

   return {"result": state["text"].upper()} # Fails if 'text' doesn't exist

Solution: Add validation or default values:

```
text = state.get("text", "")

return {"result": text.upper()}
```

Debugging Techniques

1. **Logging at Each Node**
   Introduce structured logging inside each node function.
   This lets you trace what data is being passed through each
   step of the graph.

Example:

```
def agent_node(state):

    print(f"[agent_node] Received state: {state}")

    return {"response": "Processed"}
```

2. **Use LangGraph Visualizer**
   LangGraph provides visualizations for flow inspection.
   Use graph.visualize() to render your graph and identify
   disconnected nodes, loops, or bottlenecks.

```
graph.visualize("flowchart.png")
```

3. **Unit Test Individual Nodes**
   Break down your graph logic and test each function
   separately. This speeds up debugging and isolates logic
   errors.

Example:

```
def test_process_node():

    input_state = {"text": "hello"}

    output = process_node(input_state)

    assert output == {"result": "HELLO"}
```

Handling Node Failures Gracefully

LangGraph allows custom error handling strategies by wrapping
node execution in try/except blocks or designing fallback paths in
the graph.

Example:

```python
def safe_node(state):

    try:

        return do_something(state)

    except Exception as e:

        print(f"[safe_node] Error: {e}")

        return {"error": str(e)}
```

You can also configure conditional paths for handling exceptions by checking for error keys in the next node.

Performance Bottlenecks

1. **Too Many Nested Loops or Redundant States**
   Overly complex feedback loops may lead to performance lags. Profile the system and simplify loops where possible.

2. **Heavy API Calls in Nodes**
   Calls to LLMs or external APIs should include timeout and retry mechanisms to prevent the entire flow from stalling.

Example:

```python
import requests


def fetch_data(state):
    try:
        response = requests.get(state["url"], timeout=5)
        return {"data": response.json()}
    except requests.Timeout:
        return {"error": "Timeout occurred"}
```

Best Practices to Prevent Issues

- Define and document node inputs/outputs clearly

- Use consistent naming conventions for state keys

- Isolate logic-heavy functions from graph logic

- Visualize and test your graphs incrementally

- Maintain a library of reusable, tested nodes

Conclusion

Troubleshooting LangGraph becomes manageable when you understand how data moves through nodes and how to isolate issues. Start small, log often, and build workflows iteratively. Over time, debugging becomes not just easier but also a natural part of the development process.

Chapter 5: Getting Started with CrewAI

CrewAI is an emerging Python-based framework that simplifies the orchestration of multi-agent LLM systems. It offers a clean abstraction around agents, tasks, and workflows, making it easier to define collaborative intelligence across a team of AI agents. Whether you're prototyping a smart assistant or building an autonomous research team, CrewAI gives you the foundation to do so quickly and effectively.

This chapter provides a practical walkthrough for getting started with CrewAI. You'll learn how to install the library, understand its key building blocks, construct your first working workflow, and see how it compares to LangGraph in terms of logic and structure.

5.1 Installing and Setting Up CrewAI

Getting started with CrewAI is a straightforward process. It's a lightweight framework built for orchestrating multi-agent systems using LLMs, and it's designed to be both intuitive and developer-friendly. In this section, we'll walk through how to install it, configure the environment, and verify that everything is working correctly.

Step 1: Environment Preparation

Make sure you have Python 3.8 or later installed. It's good practice to create a virtual environment to isolate dependencies:

```
python3 -m venv crewai-env
source crewai-env/bin/activate  # On Windows use
`.\crewai-env\Scripts\activate`
```

Step 2: Installing CrewAI

You can install CrewAI directly from PyPI:

```
pip install crewai
```

CrewAI depends on langchain, openai, and other libraries under the hood, so it will pull those in automatically. However, if you plan to use OpenAI's models, make sure to explicitly install the OpenAI SDK as well:

```
pip install openai
```

Step 3: Setting API Keys

CrewAI uses OpenAI under the hood for its LLMs, so you need to set your OpenAI API key. The recommended approach is to store it as an environment variable:

```
export OPENAI_API_KEY="your-api-key"  # macOS/Linux
set OPENAI_API_KEY="your-api-key"    # Windows (CMD)
$env:OPENAI_API_KEY="your-api-key"   # Windows
(PowerShell)
```

Alternatively, you can set it directly in your Python code for quick testing:

```
import os
os.environ["OPENAI_API_KEY"] = "your-api-key"
```

Step 4: Verifying the Installation

To confirm CrewAI is working, you can run a basic script that initializes a single agent and performs a simple task. Here's a minimal test:

```
from crewai import Agent, Task, Crew
from langchain.chat_models import ChatOpenAI

llm = ChatOpenAI()

agent = Agent(
    role="Tester",
    goal="Echo a test message",
```

```python
    backstory="An LLM agent set up to verify CrewAI
installation.",
    llm=llm
)

task = Task(
    description="Repeat the phrase: 'CrewAI is working
correctly.'",
    agent=agent
)

crew = Crew(
    agents=[agent],
    tasks=[task]
)

output = crew.kickoff()
print(output)
```

This simple script creates an agent, assigns it a task, and runs it within a Crew. If you see a valid response printed out, your setup is complete.

Step 5: Optional Dependencies and Tooling

Depending on the complexity of your workflow, you might want to install additional libraries like:

- chromadb or pinecone-client for vector store integration

- langchainhub if you're leveraging prebuilt chains or tools

- python-dotenv to manage environment variables from a .env file

You can install them as needed:

pip install chromadb pinecone-client python-dotenv

Personal Insight

When I first started experimenting with CrewAI, what impressed me most was how quickly I could spin up functional multi-agent systems. Unlike more complex graph-based orchestration tools, CrewAI abstracts a lot of that away—perfect for prototyping. That said, its simplicity doesn't mean it lacks power. With thoughtful agent roles and task chaining, you can get surprisingly robust behavior with very little boilerplate.

5.2 Key Concepts: Agents, Tasks, Roles, Crew

Before you can build effective workflows with CrewAI, it's essential to understand the building blocks it provides. These include **Agents**, **Tasks**, **Roles**, and the overarching structure known as the **Crew**. Each of these components contributes to creating intelligent, autonomous, and collaborative multi-agent systems.

Let's break each one down and look at how they fit together in practice.

Agents

An Agent in CrewAI is an autonomous unit powered by an LLM. Each agent is given a specific **role**, a **goal**, and some **context** or **backstory**. The idea is to encapsulate domain-specific behavior in an isolated, reusable entity.

Here's how you define a simple Agent:

```
from crewai import Agent
from langchain.chat_models import ChatOpenAI

llm = ChatOpenAI()

researcher = Agent(
    role="Researcher",
    goal="Find the latest trends in AI research",
    backstory="An experienced AI research analyst keeping track of
cutting-edge developments.",
    llm=llm
```

```
)
```

Key parameters:

- role: The function or expertise of the agent (e.g., "Researcher", "Writer", "Reviewer")

- goal: A high-level objective the agent is trying to achieve

- backstory: Additional context that helps the LLM understand how the agent should behave

- llm: The language model powering the agent (e.g., ChatOpenAI, Claude, etc.)

You can customize the model or even wrap it in tools or memory chains later for more advanced behavior.

Tasks

Tasks define **what** an agent is supposed to do. Unlike the broader "goal" field in the agent, a Task provides a specific instruction or step.

```
from crewai import Task

task = Task(
```

```
    description="Summarize the top three trends in current AI
research.",
    expected_output="A concise summary of recent AI research
trends.",
    agent=researcher
)
```

Key parameters:

- description: What the task is about

- expected_output: (Optional) What a successful output
  should look like

- agent: The agent assigned to this task

This tight mapping of agent to task allows for a clear flow of
responsibility in your workflow.

Roles

Although you pass the role as a string when defining an agent, it
plays a more critical part in shaping the agent's tone and
approach. CrewAI treats the role as a guiding persona, which the
LLM uses to adapt its response style and decision-making.

For example, a "Data Scientist" agent will behave differently from a "Journalist" agent, even when given the same task. These roles are particularly effective when used with multi-agent collaboration, ensuring diversity of expertise and perspective.

Tip: Think of roles like cast members in a film—each with a script and a personality.

Crew

The Crew is the orchestrator that brings agents and tasks together. It's responsible for executing tasks in the right order, managing agent interactions, and producing the final output of the workflow.

Here's how to assemble a basic Crew:

```
from crewai import Crew

crew = Crew(
    agents=[researcher],
    tasks=[task]
)

result = crew.kickoff()
print(result)
```

How Crew Works:

- Assigns tasks to the appropriate agents

- Manages execution in sequence or parallel (depending on task setup)

- Handles context passing and output aggregation

Putting It All Together

Let's look at a simple end-to-end setup:

```
from crewai import Agent, Task, Crew
from langchain.chat_models import ChatOpenAI

llm = ChatOpenAI()

# Define agents
researcher = Agent(
    role="AI Researcher",
    goal="Identify emerging trends in generative AI",
    backstory="An expert in AI research with years of academic and
industrial experience.",
    llm=llm
)

writer = Agent(
    role="Technical Writer",
```

```python
    goal="Communicate technical insights clearly",
    backstory="A skilled communicator with a knack for turning
complex research into digestible summaries.",
    llm=llm
)

# Define tasks
research_task = Task(
    description="Research and list three emerging trends in
generative AI.",
    agent=researcher
)

writeup_task = Task(
    description="Write a blog post summarizing these trends for a
general audience.",
    agent=writer
)

# Define crew
crew = Crew(
    agents=[researcher, writer],
    tasks=[research_task, writeup_task]
)

output = crew.kickoff()
print(output)
```

This small example shows how roles, tasks, and agents come together within a Crew to create a simple yet effective collaborative pipeline.

Personal Insight

One of the most empowering aspects of working with CrewAI is how quickly you can go from an idea to a working system. The explicit separation of concerns—roles, tasks, and agents—keeps things organized. I found it especially helpful in educational and content generation projects, where multiple perspectives and expertise levels need to come together.

As you grow your use of CrewAI, these concepts will become the foundation for more advanced workflows involving chained tasks, memory, and tool integration. Up next, we'll look at creating your first full CrewAI workflow.

5.3 Writing Your First CrewAI Workflow

Now that you understand the key building blocks—agents, tasks, roles, and crews—let's create your first working CrewAI workflow from scratch. We'll walk through everything from setup to execution in a real-world example: generating a short blog post on the latest AI trends.

Step 1: Install CrewAI

Make sure you have the crewai package installed. If not, install it using pip:

pip install crewai

Also install LangChain and your preferred LLM wrapper, such as OpenAI:

pip install openai langchain

And set your OpenAI API key as an environment variable:

export OPENAI_API_KEY="your-key-here"

Step 2: Define Your LLM

CrewAI relies on LangChain-compatible LLMs. Here we use ChatOpenAI from LangChain:

from langchain.chat_models import ChatOpenAI

llm = ChatOpenAI(temperature=0.7)

Adjust the temperature for creativity (higher = more creative, lower = more factual).

Step 3: Create Agents

Now define the agents. You'll need at least two for this workflow: one to gather insights and another to write them up.

```python
from crewai import Agent

researcher = Agent(
    role="AI Researcher",
    goal="Discover recent breakthroughs in artificial intelligence",
    backstory="An AI analyst with deep expertise in the latest research papers and industry news",
    llm=llm
)

writer = Agent(
    role="Content Writer",
    goal="Craft compelling blog articles based on research insights",
    backstory="A skilled communicator passionate about making complex ideas understandable",
    llm=llm
)
```

The backstory isn't just decoration—it shapes how the LLM responds, so give each agent a meaningful identity.

Step 4: Define Tasks

Each agent is assigned a specific task. Tasks are the actions the agent will carry out during the workflow.

```
from crewai import Task

research_task = Task(
    description="Identify and summarize three of the most recent trends in artificial intelligence",
    expected_output="A bullet-point list describing three trends with brief explanations",
    agent=researcher
)

writing_task = Task(
    description="Write a 500-word blog post explaining these trends to a general tech audience",
    expected_output="A clear, engaging, and informative blog post with a title and sections",
    agent=writer
)
```

The expected_output helps guide the agent toward the kind of response you want. This is optional but very useful for consistency.

Step 5: Assemble the Crew

With agents and tasks defined, bring them together into a crew:

```
from crewai import Crew
```

```
crew = Crew(
    agents=[researcher, writer],
    tasks=[research_task, writing_task]
)
```

This setup runs tasks in the order they are defined, passing outputs between agents if needed.

Step 6: Run the Workflow

Now, you can run the crew and see the output:

```
result = crew.kickoff()
print(result)
```

The first task (research) executes and its output becomes part of the context for the second task (writing), enabling smooth collaboration.

Example Output (Truncated)

Trend 1: AI-generated code copilots...
Trend 2: Multimodal models integrating vision and language...
Trend 3: Emergent behavior in large-scale models...

Blog Title: Top 3 Trends Shaping AI in 2025

[Full blog content...]

Final Thoughts

Writing your first workflow is straightforward, but don't underestimate the power of small refinements. Fine-tuning roles, breaking down tasks more granularly, and using tools or memory will take your agents to the next level. My personal recommendation—always test one piece at a time and inspect intermediate outputs. It'll save you hours of debugging when workflows scale.

5.4 Task Chaining and Context Propagation

One of CrewAI's biggest strengths lies in its ability to chain tasks and pass context between agents. This allows for smooth, coherent collaboration across multiple agents, each contributing specialized knowledge or skills. Whether you're building a research assistant, a customer service bot, or a content production crew, chaining tasks properly ensures consistency, accuracy, and purpose throughout the workflow.

What Is Task Chaining?

Task chaining refers to structuring tasks so that the output of one feeds into the input of another. This mimics how human teams operate: one person gathers information, another processes it, and a third builds on the results. In CrewAI, this is handled implicitly through task execution order and context sharing.

What Is Context Propagation?

Context propagation is the mechanism that passes relevant information—typically outputs of completed tasks—into subsequent tasks. This enables downstream agents to understand what's already been done, making them more effective and aligned.

CrewAI handles context propagation under the hood. However, you can improve performance by carefully structuring your expected outputs and agent prompts to ensure the context flows meaningfully.

Step-by-Step Example: Multi-Agent Report Generator

Let's build a simple 3-agent system:

- Researcher: Finds current AI news

- Analyst: Interprets the findings

- Writer: Crafts a final report

1. Define the LLM

from langchain.chat_models import ChatOpenAI

llm = ChatOpenAI(temperature=0.3)

2. Create Agents

from crewai import Agent

researcher = Agent(
    role="AI News Researcher",
    goal="Find the top 3 latest stories in AI",
    backstory="Specializes in scanning tech news for trends and breakthroughs",
    llm=llm

```python
)

analyst = Agent(
    role="AI Trends Analyst",
    goal="Analyze AI news and extract strategic insights",
    backstory="A former data scientist who focuses on evaluating
AI trends",
    llm=llm
)

writer = Agent(
    role="Technical Content Writer",
    goal="Write a structured executive summary from the analysis",
    backstory="A professional writer who creates reports from
technical material",
    llm=llm
)
```

3. Create Tasks with Expected Outputs

```python
from crewai import Task

research_task = Task(
    description="Identify the three most important news items in
AI this week",
    expected_output="A bullet-point list with source links and
short summaries",
```

```python
    agent=researcher
)

analysis_task = Task(
    description="Analyze the research findings and derive strategic
insights",
    expected_output="Three strategic insights with implications
for business or technology",
    agent=analyst
)

writing_task = Task(
    description="Write a clear, professional summary of the
findings and insights",
    expected_output="An executive summary report combining
research and analysis",
    agent=writer
)
```

Note how the expected output of one task becomes the implicit input for the next. This is the essence of task chaining.

4. Set Up the Crew

```python
from crewai import Crew

crew = Crew(
```

```
    agents=[researcher, analyst, writer],
    tasks=[research_task, analysis_task, writing_task]
)
```

Tasks are executed in order, and CrewAI handles the transfer of output context between them automatically.

5. Run the Workflow
```
result = crew.kickoff()
print(result)
```

This will produce a structured report where the writer's output is based on insights generated from both the research and the analysis.

Pro Tips for Better Chaining

- **Structure your outputs**: The clearer and more structured your expected_output, the easier it is for the next task to interpret and build on.

- **Prompt awareness**: Mention explicitly in your agent's prompt that they should read and use the results of previous tasks.

- **Debug incrementally**: Start with two tasks, ensure the context flows well, then add complexity.

Summary

Task chaining and context propagation make CrewAI a practical solution for building intelligent, collaborative workflows. You don't need to manually script data transfer between agents—CrewAI handles that, as long as your tasks are logically connected and clearly described. If you've worked with LangGraph before, think of this as a more declarative approach to state transitions, where the structure of your task list and the capabilities of your agents guide the logic.

5.5 Differences from LangGraph in Workflow Logic

LangGraph and CrewAI are both excellent frameworks for building multi-agent workflows, but their design philosophies and operational logic differ significantly. Understanding these distinctions helps you choose the right tool for the job and even combine them when appropriate.

Structural vs Declarative Logic

LangGraph is **structural** in nature. You define a graph explicitly with states, nodes, and edges. You have to model control flow—like loops, branches, and cycles—just as you would in a flowchart or a traditional programming workflow.

CrewAI, on the other hand, is **declarative**. You define agents and tasks, assign who does what, and CrewAI handles the orchestration behind the scenes. This makes it feel more natural and readable, especially for simpler workflows or when you want fast iterations.

Control Flow

LangGraph gives you fine-grained control over routing and execution. You define logic such as:

- Conditional branching based on task results

- Recursive loops for iterative refinement

- Parallel node execution and synchronization

CrewAI doesn't expose this level of control explicitly. Instead, tasks run sequentially, and context is propagated through expected outputs. If you need complex feedback loops, you'd either need to write custom logic or consider LangGraph.

Modularity and Reusability

LangGraph is modular by design. Each node in the graph is a composable function, often with reusable logic. You can refactor pieces easily, wrap them into reusable components, and plug them into different graphs.

CrewAI promotes reuse through agent definitions and task templates, but its primary strength lies in **rapid prototyping** of workflows rather than deep customization. That said, it's improving quickly and allows injecting custom functions or tools when needed.

Memory Handling

LangGraph supports custom memory modules, often plugged into specific nodes, allowing fine-tuned control over what gets remembered and when. This is useful for agent simulations, recursive summarization, or stateful interactions over time.

CrewAI handles memory implicitly via context propagation, and while this works well for linear flows, it's harder to manage state if you need granular control. However, you can manually inject memory or shared context through task output structuring or by using external tools like vector databases.

Execution Style

LangGraph is great when you're modeling **flows** that resemble algorithms—where you want explicit loops, conditions, and multi-step sequences. It's ideal for structured pipelines, simulations, and AI workflows that mimic software logic.

CrewAI shines when you're modeling **teams**—where agents with distinct goals collaborate to achieve a broader objective. It feels more like managing a team of freelancers who read briefs, complete tasks, and build on each other's work.

Example Comparison

LangGraph: Conditional Agent Routing

```
# Define logic to send to agent_a or agent_b based on topic

def router(state):

    if "finance" in state["topic"]:

        return "agent_a"

    else:

        return "agent_b"
```

You control the flow using router logic and explicitly connect states to nodes.

CrewAI: Sequential Task Assignment

```
task1 = Task(

    description="Analyze latest finance news",

    expected_output="Key findings",

    agent=finance_agent

)


task2 = Task(

    description="Summarize key findings for executive",

    expected_output="Short summary",

    agent=summary_agent

)
```

Here, the flow is determined by task order; routing is implicit.

Which Should You Use?

- Use **LangGraph** when you need:

  - Fine-grained control over logic and memory

  - Complex workflows with branching and loops

  - Reusability and programmatic orchestration

- Use **CrewAI** when you want:

  - Simpler, linear collaboration between agents

  - Fast prototyping of team-style workflows

  - Easier onboarding and readable structures

Chapter 6: Advanced CrewAI Architectures

6.1 Collaborative Planning and Role Assignment

Effective collaboration lies at the heart of building powerful multi-agent systems with CrewAI. A crew is only as strong as its agents and how well their roles and responsibilities are defined. Collaborative planning and role assignment ensure that tasks are executed efficiently, with minimal duplication and maximum synergy.

Understanding Collaboration in CrewAI

In CrewAI, collaboration is structured. Agents are designed to work together toward a common objective. This is made possible by defining a clear plan, distributing tasks based on capabilities, and assigning appropriate roles to each agent. Each role encapsulates behavior patterns, responsibilities, and decision-making authority.

Key Components of Collaborative Planning

1. **Objective Definition**
    Start by clearly outlining the desired end goal. For

example, if you're building a research crew, your goal might be to produce a summarized report based on a topic.

2. **Task Breakdown**
   Break the objective into manageable, discrete tasks. Tasks should be as atomic as possible to improve clarity and reduce confusion.

3. **Agent Capability Matching**
   Design agents with unique strengths. For instance, one agent might be proficient in data collection, another in summarization, and another in formatting results. Matching tasks to capabilities ensures optimal performance.

4. **Role Assignment**
   Roles help standardize agent behaviors across different workflows. A "Researcher" agent role may include tools for web scraping and summarization, while an "Analyst" role could focus on interpreting data.

Example: Setting Roles in Code

```
from crewai import Agent, Task, Crew

# Define agents with specific roles
```

```python
researcher = Agent(
    role='Researcher',
    goal='Collect the latest news articles on generative AI',
    backstory='A tech-savvy journalist skilled at rapid online research',
    tools=['serper', 'browser'],
)

analyst = Agent(
    role='Analyst',
    goal='Analyze and summarize findings from collected articles',
    backstory='A data analyst with a knack for pattern recognition and summarization',
)

# Assign tasks
research_task = Task(
    description='Find 5 recent articles on generative AI developments',
    expected_output='A list of article URLs and summaries',
    agent=researcher
)

analysis_task = Task(
    description='Analyze collected data and summarize key trends',
    expected_output='A bullet-point report of main takeaways',
    agent=analyst
```

```
)

# Define crew
crew = Crew(
    agents=[researcher, analyst],
    tasks=[research_task, analysis_task],
    verbose=True
)

crew.kickoff()
```

Best Practices for Role Assignment

- **Avoid Overlap**: Ensure agents don't have overlapping responsibilities unless redundancy is deliberate.

- **Create Reusable Roles**: Think modularly. Design roles that can be reused across different workflows.

- **Balance Workload**: Monitor and balance task assignments to avoid bottlenecks or idle agents.

- **Incorporate Feedback Loops**: Let agents evaluate or enhance each other's outputs where needed.

Insights from Practice

During one of my early prototypes, I created a crew where every agent could do everything. While it seemed flexible, the result was chaotic—conflicting decisions, duplicated efforts, and an unstructured flow. Only after introducing role clarity and defined responsibilities did the system begin to function as intended. The improvement in task completion time and quality was immediate.

Conclusion

Collaborative planning and role assignment are critical for the success of any CrewAI deployment. With clear goals, modular roles, and thoughtfully designed task flows, your agents will not only work together but amplify each other's strengths. This structure makes your workflows more maintainable, reusable, and scalable.

6.2 Specialized Agents and Tool Usage

As your CrewAI workflows grow more complex, generalist agents quickly hit their limits. That's where specialization becomes essential. Specialized agents are designed to perform specific functions with higher accuracy, better speed, and contextual awareness. Pair them with the right tools, and you unlock powerful capabilities that mirror real-world expert teams.

Why Specialize Agents?

Specialized agents enable you to modularize functionality, debug faster, scale easily, and ensure more predictable outputs. For example, an agent trained to extract structured data from web pages will consistently outperform a generalist agent trying to both browse, summarize, and format.

Defining Specialization

Specialization comes in a few forms:

- **Skill-based**: An agent is designed to perform a particular task type—e.g., summarization, translation, coding.

- **Domain-based**: An agent focuses on a specific domain—e.g., legal, finance, healthcare.

- **Tool-based**: An agent is tightly coupled with a particular tool or set of tools—e.g., a vector search agent using Chroma or a web scraping agent using Serper.

Example: Creating Specialized Agents

Let's walk through a setup with three specialized agents, each using tools aligned with their role.

from crewai import Agent, Task, Crew

```python
from tools import SerperTool, CalculatorTool,
ChromaSearchTool


# Research agent with web search capabilities

research_agent = Agent(

    role='Research Specialist',

    goal='Find accurate information about recent AI model
releases',

    backstory='An expert at using web tools to surface the latest
information',

    tools=[SerperTool()]

)


# Data analyst with numerical skills

analytics_agent = Agent(

    role='Data Analyst',

    goal='Analyze performance benchmarks from recent AI
papers',
```

```python
    backstory='Experienced in statistical reasoning and number crunching',

    tools=[CalculatorTool()]

)


# Memory agent for context referencing

memory_agent = Agent(

    role='Knowledge Archivist',

    goal='Reference previous findings using vector search',

    backstory='Manages and queries long-term memory for historical context',

    tools=[ChromaSearchTool()]

)
```

Assigning Tasks to Specialized Agents

```python
task1 = Task(
```

```
    description='Search for the top 3 AI models released in the last
month',

    expected_output='A short list with names, developers, and
release dates',

    agent=research_agent

)


task2 = Task(

    description='Analyze benchmark scores and identify the
highest-performing model',

    expected_output='Performance comparison and recommended
model',

    agent=analytics_agent

)


task3 = Task(

    description='Compare current models with those released in
the past six months',
```

```
    expected_output='A summary contrasting key performance
metrics over time',
                     .
    agent=memory_agent

)
```

Running the Crew

```
crew = Crew(

   agents=[research_agent, analytics_agent, memory_agent],

   tasks=[task1, task2, task3],

   verbose=True

)



crew.kickoff()
```

Tool Selection Tips

- Match tools with agent roles directly. A research agent
  doesn't need a calculator, and a math agent won't benefit

from a browser.

- Prefer agents with one or two tools to reduce cognitive load during task execution.

- Build tools modularly so they can be reused across multiple agents with similar needs.

Personal Insight

When I started using CrewAI for document processing, I initially gave all agents access to the same large set of tools. I thought more tools meant more flexibility, but it actually caused decision fatigue for the agents, leading to erratic outputs. Specializing agents and narrowing their toolsets improved performance dramatically.

Conclusion

Specialized agents backed by the right tools can outperform generalists in accuracy, speed, and consistency. Structuring your CrewAI workflows with clear specialization and tightly scoped tools leads to cleaner task delegation, easier debugging, and higher-quality results. Treat agents like domain experts, and you'll see workflows scale naturally.

6.3 Parallel Execution, Coordination, and Aggregation

When building scalable CrewAI workflows, optimizing for speed and structure becomes essential. That's where parallel execution and intelligent coordination come into play. Instead of having agents complete tasks sequentially, you can split up work streams, run them simultaneously, and then aggregate their outputs to produce a cohesive result. This approach mimics how real-world teams operate—distributing responsibilities to get more done, faster.

Understanding Parallel Execution

Parallel execution allows multiple agents to work on different tasks at the same time. CrewAI handles this internally using Python's asyncio capabilities. This pattern is especially useful when tasks are independent and don't require one another's outputs.

Example: Running Independent Tasks in Parallel

Let's create a crew with three agents, each assigned to a different research topic.

```
from crewai import Agent, Task, Crew

from tools import SerperTool
```

```
# Define agents
```

```python
ai_agent = Agent(

    role='AI Researcher',

    goal='Explore recent developments in artificial intelligence',

    tools=[SerperTool()]

)


bio_agent = Agent(

    role='Biotech Analyst',

    goal='Investigate breakthroughs in biotechnology',

    tools=[SerperTool()]

)


energy_agent = Agent(

    role='Energy Sector Expert',

    goal='Report on clean energy innovations',

    tools=[SerperTool()]
```

```python
)


# Define tasks

task_ai = Task(

    description='Find the most important AI research paper
released this month',

    agent=ai_agent

)


task_bio = Task(

    description='Summarize the latest biotech discovery that could
impact healthcare',

    agent=bio_agent

)


task_energy = Task(
```

```
    description='Identify new trends in solar and wind energy from
credible sources',

    agent=energy_agent

)



# Run tasks in parallel

crew = Crew(

    agents=[ai_agent, bio_agent, energy_agent],

    tasks=[task_ai, task_bio, task_energy],

    verbose=True

)



crew.kickoff()
```

Each agent works on its task concurrently, reducing total processing time.

Coordinating Outputs

Parallel execution is only part of the picture. Once agents complete their work, the next challenge is coordinating and combining their findings into something usable. This is where aggregation steps in.

A simple strategy is to create a fourth agent whose role is to synthesize the outputs of others. This "aggregator" receives context from the previous steps and produces a final, unified summary.

Example: Aggregating Parallel Outputs

```
from crewai_tools import FileStorageTool


synthesizer = Agent(

    role='Insights Synthesizer',

    goal='Consolidate multiple research reports into one cohesive briefing',

    tools=[FileStorageTool()]

)


aggregation_task = Task(
```

```
    description='Read outputs from previous agents and
summarize into a single executive briefing',

    agent=synthesizer

)



crew.tasks.append(aggregation_task)

crew.agents.append(synthesizer)



crew.kickoff()
```

In this setup, the synthesizer agent could read outputs from a shared storage tool or shared memory object. CrewAI also allows for lightweight context passing using the context object available in each task.

Tips for Successful Parallel Workflows

- **Keep tasks independent**: Tasks running in parallel should not rely on outputs from each other.

- **Use context only when needed**: Avoid context bloat—only pass what's essential.

- **Design for determinism**: Agents should be specialized and predictable in their behavior to reduce coordination errors.

- **Start small**: Add one or two parallel agents first, test them, and scale gradually.

Personal Insight

I once built a workflow to summarize multiple technical whitepapers. Initially, I had a single agent read all the documents one after the other. Execution time was slow and outputs lacked depth. Switching to a setup with multiple agents analyzing documents in parallel, followed by a summarizer agent, cut processing time in half and improved clarity dramatically.

Conclusion

Parallel execution combined with intelligent coordination and aggregation can significantly enhance the performance and scalability of your CrewAI systems. By dividing work across specialized agents and consolidating their outputs effectively, you build faster, smarter, and more modular multi-agent systems that align with real-world productivity strategies.

6.4 Case Study: Automated Market Analysis Crew

Building a crew that automatically analyzes market trends, competitor performance, and product sentiment can save hours of manual research. This section walks through how to set up a multi-agent system using CrewAI to automate a market analysis pipeline.

Objective

The goal is to build a crew that can:

1. Scrape and summarize financial news

2. Analyze competitor performance

3. Extract customer sentiment from reviews

4. Aggregate insights into a market intelligence report

This use case simulates what a business analyst or product strategist might do manually, but powered by agents that can work simultaneously and collaboratively.

Step 1: Define Agents

Start by setting up four agents, each responsible for a different part of the pipeline.

```
from crewai import Agent

from tools import SerperTool, NewsTool, SentimentTool


news_agent = Agent(

    role='Market News Analyst',

    goal='Summarize the most relevant financial and business news',

    tools=[NewsTool()]

)


competitor_agent = Agent(

    role='Competitor Analyst',

    goal='Monitor and summarize competitor activities',

    tools=[SerperTool()]

)
```

```
sentiment_agent = Agent(

    role='Sentiment Researcher',

    goal='Analyze customer sentiment from product reviews and
social media',

    tools=[SentimentTool()]

)




report_writer = Agent(

    role='Report Writer',

    goal='Aggregate all findings into a clear and actionable market
report'

)
```

Each agent is equipped with tools relevant to its task. These tools
might connect to APIs like Serper (Google search), news
aggregators, or sentiment analysis libraries.

Step 2: Define Tasks

Next, create tasks aligned with each agent's responsibility. Tasks describe what needs to be done, and the agent handles how to do it.

from crewai import Task

task_news = Task(

   description='Gather and summarize today's top business and finance news',

   agent=news_agent

)

task_competitor = Task(

   description='Identify key moves from top 3 competitors in the last week',

   agent=competitor_agent

)

```python
task_sentiment = Task(

    description='Extract and analyze customer reviews to identify
product sentiment',

    agent=sentiment_agent

)


task_report = Task(

    description='Compile findings from all tasks into a single
executive summary',

    agent=report_writer

)
```

These tasks should reflect real analyst goals so the output mimics
something you'd present to stakeholders.

Step 3: Assemble and Run the Crew

Combine the agents and tasks into a crew and run the pipeline.

```python
from crewai import Crew
```

```
crew = Crew(

    agents=[news_agent, competitor_agent, sentiment_agent,
report_writer],

    tasks=[task_news, task_competitor, task_sentiment,
task_report],

    verbose=True

)



result = crew.kickoff()

print(result)
```

This will trigger all agents to perform their tasks. Tasks that don't rely on previous output run in parallel, while the report-writing task waits until the rest are complete.

Step 4: Customize Aggregation Logic (Optional)

If you want more control over how the final report is written, you can pass structured outputs from earlier agents into the report writer's context.

```
task_report.context = {

    'news': task_news.output,

    'competitors': task_competitor.output,

    'sentiment': task_sentiment.output

}
```

This can help the final agent structure its output better, ensuring each section is clearly defined.

6.5 Tips for Scalable CrewAI Deployments

Scaling a CrewAI deployment means moving beyond local experiments to robust workflows that can serve real-world applications with reliability and performance. Whether you're running on a single machine or scaling across distributed infrastructure, careful design and infrastructure planning will determine the success of your multi-agent systems.

1. Use Stateless Agents with Context Passing

Design agents to be stateless. Instead of relying on memory persistence within the agent, explicitly pass required context through tasks. This makes it easier to parallelize execution and improves reliability when scaling across systems.

```python
from crewai import Task


task = Task(

    description="Write a report using the context provided",

    agent=report_writer,

    context={

        "news_summary": news_output,

        "competitor_updates": competitor_output,

        "customer_sentiment": sentiment_output

    }
)
```

Keeping data flow explicit also simplifies debugging and allows better logging.

2. Minimize Agent Overlap with Clear Roles

To prevent redundancy and increase parallel execution, define roles that are sharply scoped. Overlapping responsibilities across agents can lead to duplicate work or conflicting outputs. Use role names and goals that are clearly distinct, such as "Technical Documentation Writer" vs. "Code Reviewer" rather than generic roles like "Developer."

3. Monitor and Log Every Stage

For large-scale deployments, logging is non-negotiable. Use structured logging for each agent's task, input, and output. CrewAI doesn't enforce a logging framework, so integrate your own using Python's built-in logging module or an external system like Sentry, Logstash, or Datadog.

```
import logging

logging.basicConfig(level=logging.INFO)


logging.info(f"Agent {agent.role} started task: {task.description}")
```

You can wrap logging inside your own custom task wrapper if you want centralized tracking.

4. Use Task Dependency Graphs for Complex Flows

Avoid manually chaining task executions in long, brittle sequences. Instead, define a task dependency graph using upstream task outputs as input context for downstream tasks. This allows for dynamic resolution, better parallelism, and less error-prone pipelines.

```
task_summary.context = {

    "research_data": task_research.output,

    "analysis_result": task_analysis.output

}
```

This technique also works well when integrating LangGraph with CrewAI for hybrid workflows.

5. Choose the Right Model for the Right Agent

Different agents may benefit from different LLM providers or models. A research summarization agent might require GPT-4, but a sentiment analyzer could perform just as well (and cheaper) with Claude or GPT-3.5. CrewAI lets you define custom models per agent if needed.

```
Agent(

    role='Lightweight Sentiment Analyst',

    goal='Quickly score sentiment on product feedback',

    model='gpt-3.5-turbo',

    tools=[...]

)
```

Optimize your deployment cost and speed by making intelligent model choices.

6. Externalize Tools and Extendability

Keep tools modular and defined outside of agent code. Tools should be reusable components that can be plugged into multiple agents. This makes it easier to test, mock, and upgrade tools independently.

```
from tools import CustomSearchTool, DataCleanerTool
```

```python
data_agent = Agent(

    role='Data Aggregator',

    goal='Collect and clean product data',

    tools=[CustomSearchTool(), DataCleanerTool()]

)
```

Avoid defining tools inline—externalizing tool logic supports better separation of concerns and faster iteration.

7. Run Agents Concurrently Where Possible

CrewAI currently supports sequential task execution, but you can parallelize agents manually with Python's asyncio or concurrent.futures when tasks are independent. This is particularly useful for agents performing data collection or enrichment in parallel.

```python
import asyncio


async def run_agent_task(agent, task):

    return await task.run()
```

```python
# Schedule concurrent execution

await asyncio.gather(

    run_agent_task(agent1, task1),

    run_agent_task(agent2, task2),

    run_agent_task(agent3, task3)

)
```

This approach significantly reduces total processing time for large-scale crews.

8. Containerize and Automate Deployment

To scale in production environments, containerize your CrewAI app using Docker. This allows you to deploy across cloud platforms like AWS, GCP, or Azure with orchestration tools like Kubernetes. It also makes local development more consistent and reproducible.

Create a simple Dockerfile:

```
FROM python:3.11
```

```
WORKDIR /app

COPY . .

RUN pip install -r requirements.txt

CMD ["python", "main.py"]
```

Then deploy using CI/CD pipelines to automate updates and deployments.

9. Handle Failures Gracefully

At scale, things will break—APIs will timeout, tools might fail, agents may return garbage. Implement try/except blocks inside your custom tools and wrap task executions with retry logic or fallback strategies.

```
try:

    result = agent.run(task)

except Exception as e:

    logging.error(f"Agent failed: {e}")

    result = "Default response due to failure"
```

This makes your system resilient and ensures one agent's failure doesn't collapse the entire workflow.

10. Cache Intermediate Results

If agents perform expensive operations like long queries or LLM completions, use caching where appropriate. Libraries like joblib, diskcache, or even Redis can help reduce costs and latency.

```python
from diskcache import Cache


cache = Cache('./cache')


def cached_llm_call(prompt):

    if prompt in cache:

        return cache[prompt]

    result = call_llm(prompt)

    cache[prompt] = result

    return result
```

Caching also supports reproducibility for audit trails and post-mortems.

Conclusion

Scaling CrewAI isn't just about throwing more agents at a problem. It requires clear task separation, well-defined agent roles, intelligent model choices, and infrastructure that can support reliability and concurrency. With these strategies, you can confidently move from prototypes to production-ready AI workflows that are fast, modular, and maintainable.

Chapter 7: Building Hybrid Systems

As multi-agent systems evolve, the real power often comes from not choosing one framework over another, but combining their strengths. LangGraph offers structured, state-driven control, ideal for directed logic and flow coordination. CrewAI excels at dynamic, role-based task delegation and collaboration. In this chapter, we'll dive into hybrid systems that blend the best of both worlds.

7.1 Combining LangGraph and CrewAI

Combining LangGraph and CrewAI can unlock powerful patterns for agent coordination, particularly when tasks require both deterministic graph-based logic and flexible role-based collaboration. Each framework brings unique capabilities that complement the other. LangGraph excels in managing control flows, state transitions, and recursive workflows. CrewAI shines when orchestrating agents with dynamic roles, tasks, and collaborative reasoning. Integrating them allows for building hybrid systems that are modular, scalable, and expressive.

Why Combine LangGraph and CrewAI?

LangGraph provides structure. It ensures workflows are predictable, traceable, and reusable. CrewAI enables intelligent teams to think collaboratively, take on roles, and solve problems through loosely coupled interactions. When combined, you can use LangGraph to route between complex decision points, manage memory across workflows, and delegate role-specific tasks to a CrewAI team.

For example, imagine a content generation pipeline: LangGraph handles input parsing, branching logic, and iterative review loops, while CrewAI agents handle research, drafting, editing, and summarization.

Hybrid Architecture Overview

To build a hybrid system:

1. **Define the LangGraph workflow** that includes edges and nodes for logic.

2. **Invoke CrewAI crews** as part of specific nodes, delegating decisions or creative work.

3. **Pass context/state between the two** using shared memory or message protocols.

Code Example: Using CrewAI within a LangGraph Node

```
1.  from langgraph.graph import StateGraph, END
2.  from crewai import Agent, Task, Crew
```

```python
3.
4.    # Define a simple CrewAI team
5.    researcher = Agent(role="Researcher", goal="Find facts
      about LangChain")
6.    writer = Agent(role="Writer", goal="Draft a concise
      explanation")
7.
8.    task1 = Task(description="Research LangChain",
      expected_output="5 facts")
9.    task2 = Task(description="Write summary based on
      facts")
10.
11.   crew = Crew(agents=[researcher, writer], tasks=[task1,
      task2])
12.   # Define a LangGraph node that runs the crew
13.   async def run_crew_node(state):
14.       results = crew.run()  # Synchronously or
      asynchronously depending on your use case
15.       state['crew_output'] = results
16.       return state
17.   # LangGraph flow
18.   workflow = StateGraph()
19.   workflow.add_node("RunCrew", run_crew_node)
20.   workflow.set_entry_point("RunCrew")
21.   workflow.set_finish_point(END)
22.   app = workflow.compile()
23.   result = app.invoke({})
```

```
24.  print(result['crew_output'])
```

Key Considerations

- **Data Passing**: Ensure that data from LangGraph is cleanly handed off to CrewAI and vice versa. Use JSON or structured objects.

- **Asynchronous Execution**: If crews are long-running, consider async integration using Python's asyncio to avoid blocking.

- **Error Handling**: Capture exceptions from CrewAI agents and handle them gracefully in LangGraph using edge transitions.

Benefits of Hybridization

- **Modularity**: Crews are reusable and independent; they can be swapped in and out of LangGraph workflows.

- **Flexibility**: You can evolve workflows without rewriting agent logic.

- **Collaboration + Control**: LangGraph gives process control; CrewAI provides team intelligence.

Personal Insight

In my projects, I often find LangGraph useful for structuring a workflow where the flow must be very explicit—like multi-step form processing or decision trees. But for creative or subjective tasks, I drop into a CrewAI node and let the agents debate, research, or brainstorm. This duality mirrors how humans often work: structure plus spontaneity.

By combining these two frameworks, you're not just building smarter workflows—you're designing digital organizations that can scale, adapt, and collaborate.

7.2 When and Why to Use a Hybrid Approach

Combining LangGraph and CrewAI unlocks the ability to design workflows that are both structured and collaborative. While each framework excels in specific contexts—LangGraph in deterministic, state-machine-like logic and CrewAI in dynamic multi-agent collaboration—a hybrid setup allows you to use the best of both worlds. But the key to a successful hybrid approach is knowing *when* and *why* to reach for it.

When to Use a Hybrid Approach

1. **Complex, Long-Running Workflows with Multiple Roles**

   If your application involves several stages of processing that each require different expertise—like research, analysis, summarization, and reporting—LangGraph can manage the overall flow while CrewAI handles task-level collaboration. For example, LangGraph might route a task to a "research crew" and then to a "summarization crew," with clear transitions and checkpointing between them.

2. **Conditional Logic with Team-Based Execution**

   LangGraph's edge logic and branching are ideal for making decisions based on intermediate results. If the outcome of one task determines which crew should handle the next step, LangGraph can evaluate the condition and dynamically assign the task to the correct crew. CrewAI alone doesn't offer this kind of high-level routing.

3. **Orchestrating Multiple Crews Sequentially or in Parallel**

   Sometimes you need to launch different crews for different parts of a project—say, a data validation team, a trend analysis team, and a strategy team. LangGraph can spin up these crews in parallel and aggregate their results. CrewAI by itself isn't optimized for this kind of graph-based orchestration.

4. **Retry Logic and Looping over Crew Output**
   LangGraph's looping and retry mechanisms allow you to reprocess data or rerun crews until a certain condition is met (e.g., "the report passes validation"). This isn't straightforward to implement using CrewAI alone.

Why It Matters

Using a hybrid setup enables you to:

- Maintain high-level control (LangGraph) while allowing flexible execution (CrewAI)

- Create workflows that are easier to debug, extend, and test

- Reduce coupling between agents and logic, improving modularity

- Combine deterministic process flows with autonomous behavior

Example: A Hybrid Workflow for Content Moderation and Publishing

Let's walk through a practical example. Say you're building a system that reviews user-generated content, flags offensive items, and publishes clean submissions to a blog.

1. **LangGraph controls the flow**:

   - Step 1: Pass the content through a validation node

   - Step 2: If flagged, send to moderation crew

   - Step 3: If approved, route to publishing crew

   - Step 4: Archive result and report to admin

2. **CrewAI handles moderation and publishing**:

   - Moderation crew might include agents for legal, ethical, and tone review

   - Publishing crew might format content, generate tags, and push it to CMS

Here's a simplified sketch of how this hybrid flow looks:

```python
from langgraph.graph import StateGraph, END

from crewai import Crew, Agent, Task


# Setup CrewAI crews
moderation_agents = [Agent(...), Agent(...)]

publishing_agents = [Agent(...), Agent(...)]


moderation_crew = Crew(

    agents=moderation_agents,

    tasks=[Task(description="Moderate content")]

)


publishing_crew = Crew(

    agents=publishing_agents,

    tasks=[Task(description="Publish content")]

)
```

```python
# LangGraph nodes

def validate_content(state):
    content = state["content"]
    if "bad word" in content:
        return {"flagged": True, "content": content}
    return {"flagged": False, "content": content}


def moderate(state):
    result = moderation_crew.run(input=state["content"])
    return {"moderated_content": result}


def publish(state):
    result = publishing_crew.run(input=state.get("moderated_content") or state["content"])
    return {"published": True, "output": result}
```

```python
builder = StateGraph(input_schema={"content": str})


builder.add_node("validate", validate_content)

builder.add_node("moderate", moderate)

builder.add_node("publish", publish)


builder.set_entry_point("validate")


builder.add_conditional_edges(

    "validate",

    lambda state: "moderate" if state["flagged"] else "publish",

    {"moderate", "publish"}

)


builder.add_edge("moderate", "publish")
```

```
builder.add_edge("publish", END)
```

```
graph = builder.compile()

result = graph.invoke({"content": "This is a clean post"})
```

Best Practices for Hybrid Design

- Keep roles clear: Let LangGraph handle control flow, and CrewAI manage teamwork

- Pass minimal, structured data between frameworks to simplify debugging

- Test each layer independently before integrating

- Use logging generously, especially when passing context between systems

A hybrid approach gives you the flexibility to architect intelligent workflows that are both disciplined and adaptive. It's like pairing a conductor with a jazz band—structure and creativity working hand-in-hand.

7.3 Shared Memory and State Transitions Across Frameworks

When building hybrid systems with LangGraph and CrewAI, one of the most important challenges—and opportunities—is managing memory and state transitions cleanly between the two frameworks. This is where things often get messy if you're not careful, but with a solid structure in place, it can also be a powerful advantage. Understanding how to move data back and forth predictably is key to keeping your workflows robust and scalable.

Why Shared State Matters

LangGraph and CrewAI each maintain their own mechanisms for passing and mutating state. LangGraph works with an explicit state object passed between nodes, while CrewAI uses input parameters and internal task state propagation across agents. If you're integrating both in a single system, you need a reliable way to hand off information between them without introducing tight coupling or confusing data flows.

This shared memory model lets you:

- Keep track of intermediate results across framework boundaries

- Store decisions or agent responses that need to influence later steps

- Enable feedback loops where LangGraph decisions are based on CrewAI output

Designing a Shared Memory Strategy

A good shared memory strategy hinges on having a unified, consistent structure for state that is passed and updated across both systems. A Python dictionary usually does the job. You can define a schema or use type hints to keep it clean.

Here's a simple shared state model:

```
state = {

 "user_query": "Summarize recent AI trends",

 "research_results": [],

 "summary_draft": "",

 "moderation_feedback": "",

 "final_output": ""

}
```

Practical Workflow: LangGraph Orchestrating CrewAI

Let's walk through a case where LangGraph drives the workflow, and CrewAI handles execution within certain steps.

1. **LangGraph controls the logic**

2. **CrewAI modifies and updates parts of the shared state**

3. **LangGraph makes routing decisions based on updated state**

Here's what that might look like:

```
from langgraph.graph import StateGraph, END

from crewai import Crew, Agent, Task



# Define some example CrewAI agents and crews

research_agent = Agent(role="Researcher", goal="Gather relevant information")
```

```python
summary_agent = Agent(role="Summarizer", goal="Create
concise summary")


research_crew = Crew(

    agents=[research_agent],

    tasks=[Task(description="Collect recent news on AI trends")]

)


summary_crew = Crew(

    agents=[summary_agent],

    tasks=[Task(description="Summarize the research findings")]

)


# Define LangGraph functions
def collect_research(state):

    research_output =
research_crew.run(input=state["user_query"])
```

```python
    state["research_results"] = research_output

    return state


def summarize(state):

    summary =
summary_crew.run(input=state["research_results"])

    state["summary_draft"] = summary

    return state


builder = StateGraph(input_schema=dict)


builder.add_node("research", collect_research)

builder.add_node("summarize", summarize)


builder.set_entry_point("research")

builder.add_edge("research", "summarize")
```

```python
builder.add_edge("summarize", END)


graph = builder.compile()


initial_state = {

  "user_query": "Summarize recent AI trends",

  "research_results": [],

  "summary_draft": ""

}


output = graph.invoke(initial_state)
```

Here, LangGraph is coordinating the flow. Each node receives and returns the state dictionary. CrewAI agents receive specific fields from the state and write results back into the same structure. This allows both systems to stay in sync without becoming tangled.

Best Practices for Shared State

- **Define a shared schema early**: Treat your state like an API. Know what fields exist and who owns them.

- **Encapsulate updates**: Use LangGraph nodes to control when and how state fields are updated by external systems like CrewAI.

- **Avoid tight coupling**: Don't let CrewAI mutate in unpredictable ways. Instead, return data explicitly and let LangGraph decide what to store.

- **Use namespacing in keys**: Prefix or nest data (e.g., state["crew"]["research_output"]) to avoid key collisions and improve clarity.

Debugging State Transitions

Logging is your friend here. At each LangGraph node, consider printing or logging the state diff to track what changed. For example:

```
import json
```

```
def log_state(state, label):
    print(f"--- {label} ---")
```

```
print(json.dumps(state, indent=2))

return state
```

This can be wrapped into each node for easy monitoring.

7.4 Dynamic Task Generation and Execution

One of the most powerful features in hybrid LangGraph and
CrewAI workflows is the ability to dynamically generate tasks
based on real-time input or intermediate results. This flexibility
allows your system to adapt to user needs, handle diverse use cases,
and build truly autonomous behavior. Whether you're dealing
with branching logic, uncertain task outcomes, or variable input
complexity, dynamically creating tasks enables intelligent
responsiveness.

What Does Dynamic Task Generation Mean?

Dynamic task generation refers to creating new agent tasks or
execution paths at runtime, not just at design time. Instead of
predefining every possible step, your workflow adapts on the
fly—often driven by earlier outputs or user interactions. For
example:

- If a query is too broad, the system can break it into subtopics.

- If the result set is large, the system can distribute summarization across multiple agents.

- Based on user feedback, it can generate follow-up research tasks.

LangGraph is particularly good at handling dynamic flow logic, while CrewAI can be used to spawn agents and tasks based on runtime information.

LangGraph + CrewAI Dynamic Task Example

Let's build a system that accepts a general user query, identifies subtopics using one agent, and then dynamically generates research tasks for each subtopic. The idea is to let the system determine how many subtasks to create—and let CrewAI agents handle the actual execution.

Step 1: Define CrewAI Agents

```
from crewai import Agent, Task, Crew



# Agent to break down general queries
```

```python
planner_agent = Agent(role="Planner", goal="Divide a broad
topic into specific subtopics")


# Research agent for executing generated tasks

research_agent = Agent(role="Researcher", goal="Conduct deep
research on a subtopic")
```

Step 2: LangGraph Functions

```python
def plan_subtopics(state):

    response = planner_agent.run(input=state["user_query"])

    subtopics = response.split("\n")  # Assume agent returns a list of
subtopics

    state["subtopics"] = [t.strip() for t in subtopics if t.strip()]

    return state


def generate_and_run_tasks(state):

    results = []
```

```python
    for topic in state["subtopics"]:

        task = Task(description=f"Research: {topic}")

        crew = Crew(agents=[research_agent], tasks=[task])

        result = crew.run()

        results.append({"topic": topic, "research": result})

    state["research_results"] = results

    return state
```

Step 3: Assemble LangGraph Workflow

```python
from langgraph.graph import StateGraph, END


builder = StateGraph(input_schema=dict)


builder.add_node("plan", plan_subtopics)
builder.add_node("research", generate_and_run_tasks)
```

```python
builder.set_entry_point("plan")

builder.add_edge("plan", "research")

builder.add_edge("research", END)


graph = builder.compile()
```

Step 4: Run the Workflow

```python
initial_state = {"user_query": "Provide insights into AI trends in education, healthcare, and finance"}


output = graph.invoke(initial_state)


for item in output["research_results"]:

    print(f"\nTopic: {item['topic']}\nResult: {item['research']}")
```

This system can scale to handle an arbitrary number of subtopics, all handled by the same research agent but on dynamically created tasks.

Dynamic Task Benefits

- **Flexibility**: You don't need to anticipate every case at build time.

- **Scalability**: Easily extend workflows to handle N tasks based on context.

- **Autonomy**: The system behaves more like a real assistant—thinking before acting.

Best Practices for Dynamic Execution

- **Use metadata in state** to track what's already been executed.

- **Make CrewAI tasks idempotent**, so reruns don't cause inconsistent results.

- **Log inputs/outputs** per task to help debug and fine-tune performance.

- **Keep subtask granularity manageable**, especially if using feedback loops.

Conclusion

Dynamic task generation bridges the gap between rigid pipelines and fluid, intelligent agents. When LangGraph determines logic and CrewAI delivers execution, you gain a hybrid model that's both powerful and maintainable. Whether you're breaking down research goals, reacting to unexpected input, or automating workflows based on changing conditions, dynamic task generation gives your agents the ability to think on their feet.

7.5 Building Autonomous Teams with Graph-Controlled Crews

Combining LangGraph's structured control flow with CrewAI's flexible, role-based agents opens the door to fully autonomous teams—groups of agents that work together, make decisions, and execute tasks independently based on a centralized logic graph. This setup is ideal for orchestrating large, multi-step workflows where agents must cooperate and adjust dynamically as new information becomes available.

This guide walks through building a graph-controlled crew that autonomously handles a multi-stage content publishing pipeline: planning, research, writing, and editorial review.

Key Concept: Graph-Controlled Crew

In this architecture:

- **LangGraph** controls flow: state transitions, branching logic, error handling, and sequence orchestration.

- **CrewAI** executes work through modular agents assigned to specific tasks, guided by roles and goals.

- **Autonomy** is enabled by encoding coordination into LangGraph's state machine, while CrewAI agents focus solely on execution.

Step-by-Step Implementation

Let's build a system where:

1. A planner decides what content to write.

2. Researchers gather facts.

3. Writers create drafts.

4. Editors refine the output.

Step 1: Define CrewAI Agents

```
from crewai import Agent, Task, Crew



planner = Agent(role="Content Planner", goal="Propose article
titles based on user interest")

researcher = Agent(role="Researcher", goal="Gather accurate
facts for a given article")

writer = Agent(role="Writer", goal="Write a compelling article
using research data")

editor = Agent(role="Editor", goal="Polish the article to ensure
readability and quality")
```

Step 2: LangGraph Nodes

Each node represents a phase in the team's operation.

```
def planning_node(state):

    response = planner.run(input=state["topic"])
```

```python
    state["titles"] = [t.strip() for t in response.split("\n") if t.strip()]

    return state


def research_node(state):

    facts = {}

    for title in state["titles"]:

        task = Task(description=f"Research for: {title}")

        crew = Crew(agents=[researcher], tasks=[task])

        result = crew.run()

        facts[title] = result

    state["facts"] = facts

    return state


def writing_node(state):

    drafts = {}

    for title, info in state["facts"].items():
```

```python
        task = Task(description=f"Write article:
{title}\nFacts:\n{info}")

        crew = Crew(agents=[writer], tasks=[task])

        result = crew.run()

        drafts[title] = result

    state["drafts"] = drafts

    return state


def editing_node(state):
    polished = {}

    for title, draft in state["drafts"].items():

        task = Task(description=f"Edit this article:\n{draft}")

        crew = Crew(agents=[editor], tasks=[task])

        result = crew.run()

        polished[title] = result

    state["final_articles"] = polished
```

```
    return state
```

Step 3: Define LangGraph State Machine

```python
from langgraph.graph import StateGraph, END


builder = StateGraph(input_schema=dict)


builder.add_node("plan", planning_node)

builder.add_node("research", research_node)

builder.add_node("write", writing_node)

builder.add_node("edit", editing_node)


builder.set_entry_point("plan")

builder.add_edge("plan", "research")

builder.add_edge("research", "write")

builder.add_edge("write", "edit")
```

```
builder.add_edge("edit", END)
```

```
graph = builder.compile()
```

Step 4: Run the System

```
input_data = {"topic": "Latest innovations in AI for climate
change"}
```

```
result = graph.invoke(input_data)
```

```
for title, article in result["final_articles"].items():

    print(f"\nTitle: {title}\n\n{article}")
```

Why This Approach Works

- **Modularity**: Each agent is isolated in its own domain, making it easier to test and update roles.

- **Traceability**: LangGraph's structured flow gives visibility into the state and transitions.

- **Autonomy**: Agents aren't micromanaged. They're assigned outcomes and operate independently within their task.

- **Scalability**: New roles (e.g., legal reviewer or social media rep) can be added by inserting nodes in the graph.

Best Practices

- **Define clear state keys** to avoid overlap and confusion between graph transitions.

- **Use LangGraph for coordination**, not execution—keep agents focused on generating or transforming content.

- **Log outputs per node** to trace results and debug when things go wrong.

- **Use conditionals or branching** in LangGraph if some articles need more research or secondary review.

Chapter 8: Agent Tools and Memory Systems

As agents evolve in complexity and scope, their capabilities need to extend beyond simple language modeling. Tools and memory systems are critical enhancements that allow agents to interact with the world, retain knowledge, and operate intelligently across long contexts and workflows. This chapter will walk through the standard tools, how to build custom ones, how vector stores support memory, and how to architect long-term context and persistence for autonomous agents.

8.1 Common Tools: Search, Code, File Readers, APIs

Equipping agents with tools is what elevates them from conversational models to practical digital workers. Tools enable agents to retrieve live data, execute code, process files, and interact with external systems via APIs. This section introduces some of the most widely used tools and shows how to integrate them into your agent workflows using LangChain or CrewAI-compatible patterns.

Why Tools Matter

LLMs can reason and generate responses, but they lack native access to real-time data, mathematical precision, or interaction with files and APIs. Tools act as extensions that bridge this gap. Think of them as skill modules agents can call on when needed.

Web Search Tools

Search tools let agents pull current data from the internet. While LLMs are trained on vast datasets, their static knowledge means they can't answer recent queries without a search capability.

```
from langchain.tools import DuckDuckGoSearchRun

from langchain.agents import Tool


search_tool = Tool(

    name="DuckDuckGo Search",

    func=DuckDuckGoSearchRun().run,

    description="Use this to fetch up-to-date information from the internet."

)
```

Agents can now answer queries like "What's the latest news about OpenAI?" by invoking the search_tool.

Python Code Execution

For numerical computation, data transformation, or logical evaluation, Python execution tools let agents run snippets of code dynamically.

from long chain.utilities import PythonREPL

from langchain.agents import Tool

python_tool = Tool(

   name="Python Executor",

   func=PythonREPL().run,

   description="Executes Python code to solve math or logical problems."

)

This is extremely useful for answering analytical questions like "What's the standard deviation of this dataset?" or converting formats between systems.

File Readers (PDF, CSV, DOCX)

Agents often need to analyze uploaded documents. File reader tools can parse and extract content from files so the agent can summarize or search them.

Here's an example using LangChain's PyMuPDFLoader for PDFs:

```python
from langchain.document_loaders import PyMuPDFLoader


loader = PyMuPDFLoader("sample.pdf")

documents = loader.load()


for doc in documents:

    print(doc.page_content[:200])  # print snippet
```

Once the document is ingested, you can pass the content to an LLM, chunk it into a vector store for semantic search, or summarize it via a prompt chain.

API Call Tools

Agents can also call APIs using standard REST interfaces. This is especially useful when integrating with internal systems, financial data feeds, or third-party platforms.

Here's a custom API tool using Python's requests:

```python
import requests

from langchain.agents import Tool


def get_weather(city):

    response = requests.get(f"https://wttr.in/{city}?format=3")

    return response.text


weather_tool = Tool(

    name="Weather Tool",
```

```
func=get_weather,

description="Returns current weather for a given city"

)
```

Now the agent can handle prompts like "What's the weather in Berlin?" using real-time API data.

Tool Integration Best Practices

From experience, here are a few rules that help when integrating tools into your agent workflows:

- Use tools sparingly. Too many tools create decision fatigue for the agent and reduce reliability.

- Write precise tool descriptions. This improves the FIRM's ability to select the right one.

- Test tool output formatting. Tools should return results the agent can interpret easily, especially if chaining is involved.

- Handle tool errors gracefully. Always wrap tools in try/except logic or return fallback responses.

Tools are the most powerful way to extend the functionality of agents. They enable access, execution, and interaction—giving agents the ability to solve real-world problems, not just talk about them.

8.2 Custom Tool Development

While built-in tools like search or Python execution are great for common use cases, many real-world workflows require custom tools tailored to specific tasks. Whether you're accessing a proprietary API, querying a database, or automating internal business logic, creating your own tool gives you precise control over the agent's capabilities.

Why Build Custom Tools?

Every organization has unique needs—custom logic, private systems, domain-specific knowledge. A generic agent won't know how to interact with these unless you explicitly teach it through a tool interface. Developing a custom tool bridges the gap between your LLM agents and your specific environment.

Anatomy of a Tool

In LangChain or CrewAI-compatible frameworks, a tool is simply a callable function with a name and a description. Here's a basic structure:

```python
from langchain.agents import Tool


def my_custom_function(input_str: str) -> str:

    # Logic to process the input

    return f"Received: {input_str}"


custom_tool = Tool(

    name="EchoTool",

    func=my_custom_function,

    description="Echoes back the input string"

)
```

The description is important—it guides the LLM in when and how to use the tool during reasoning.

Example: Internal Company API Tool

Let's build a tool that queries an internal HR API to fetch employee profiles based on name or ID.

```python
import requests

from langchain.agents import Tool


def get_employee_profile(name: str) -> str:
    try:
        response = requests.get(f"https://internal.api/employees?name={name}")

        if response.status_code == 200:

            data = response.json()

            return f"{data['name']} - {data['role']} - {data['department']}"

        else:

            return "Employee not found"

    except Exception as e:

        return f"Error: {str(e)}"
```

```
employee_tool = Tool(

    name="Employee Lookup",

    func=get_employee_profile,

    description="Use this to find employee details by name"

)
```

Agents can now answer queries like "What department does John Smith work in?" with live backend data.

Adding Input Parsing and Validation

LLMs are good at language, but your tool might need structured input. You can create pre-processing logic to validate or convert the LLM's output.

```
def get_stock_quote(input_str: str) -> str:

    symbol = input_str.strip().upper()

    if not symbol.isalpha():

        return "Invalid stock symbol"
```

```python
    response =
requests.get(f"https://api.example.com/stocks/{symbol}")

    if response.status_code == 200:

        data = response.json()

        return f"{symbol}: ${data['price']}"

    return "Stock not found"
```

Tool Wrapping for Enhanced Logging or Monitoring

In production settings, I often wrap tools with decorators for logging or telemetry. This helps track usage, debug errors, or monitor performance.

```python
def logging_wrapper(func):

    def wrapper(input_str):

        print(f"Tool called with: {input_str}")

        result = func(input_str)

        print(f"Tool returned: {result}")
```

```python
        return result

    return wrapper


@logging_wrapper

def simple_math_tool(input_str: str) -> str:

    try:

        return str(eval(input_str))

    except:

        return "Invalid math expression"
```

Registering Custom Tools with Agents

Once the tool is defined, include it in the agent's list of available tools:

```python
from langchain.agents import initialize_agent, AgentType

from langchain.chat_models import ChatOpenAI
```

```
agent = initialize_agent(

    tools=[employee_tool],

    llm=ChatOpenAI(),

    agent=AgentType.ZERO_SHOT_REACT_DESCRIPTION,

    verbose=True

)
```

Now the agent can choose the employee_tool as part of its reasoning process based on user prompts.

Design Tips for Effective Tools

- Keep tools focused. One tool = one purpose.

- Be specific with names and descriptions.

- Always handle input/output formatting and edge cases.

- Monitor tool usage to identify confusion or misuse.

The more aligned your tools are with the agent's goals, the more capable and intelligent the overall system becomes. Custom tool development is where the magic happens—it's how you operationalize LLMs for your business context.

8.3 Using Vector Stores for Agent Memory

As agents become more capable, their effectiveness depends on how well they can recall, reference, and use past information. Vector stores provide a powerful mechanism to store and retrieve rich semantic content using embeddings, making them ideal for augmenting agent memory in dynamic workflows.

What Is a Vector Store?

A vector store holds high-dimensional embeddings—numerical representations of text generated by models like OpenAI's text-embedding-ada-002. Instead of matching words or phrases, a vector store retrieves information based on meaning, allowing agents to access relevant knowledge even if it's phrased differently from the query.

Use Cases for Vector Stores in Agent Memory

- Storing conversation history for long-term memory

- Retrieving documentation or knowledge base articles

- Personalizing agent behavior with user-specific data

- Maintaining contextual awareness across tasks

Getting Started with FAISS and LangChain

LangChain supports multiple vector stores, but FAISS is one of the most accessible for local development. Here's how to set it up.

pip install faiss-cpu langchain openai

Step 1: Generate Embeddings

First, use an embedding model to convert text into vectors.

from langchain.embeddings import OpenAIEmbeddings

embedding_model = OpenAIEmbeddings()

texts = ["LangGraph handles state machines.", "CrewAI organizes agent collaboration."]

```
embeddings = embedding_model.embed_documents(texts)
```

Step 2: Create the Vector Store

Use FAISS to build an index of these embeddings.

```
from langchain.vectorstores import FAISS
```

```
vectorstore = FAISS.from_texts(texts, embedding_model)
```

Now, the store can match new queries semantically against the indexed data.

Step 3: Querying the Vector Store

Let's search for a relevant chunk based on a user question.

```
query = "How do agents coordinate in CrewAI?"

result = vectorstore.similarity_search(query, k=1)

print(result[0].page_content)
```

The output will return the most semantically similar text snippet—even if the wording differs from the original.

Step 4: Integrating with an Agent

To make the vector store part of an agent's reasoning loop, wrap it in a retrieval tool.

```
from langchain.tools import Tool


def crew_memory_search(query: str) -> str:

    results = vectorstore.similarity_search(query, k=2)

    return "\n".join([r.page_content for r in results])


memory_tool = Tool(

    name="CrewMemory",

    func=crew_memory_search,

    description="Retrieve relevant info about agent coordination using semantic search"

)
```

Now, the agent can call CrewMemory just like any other tool to ground its answers in stored knowledge.

Step 5: Dynamically Updating the Store

As agents interact with users or generate new knowledge, you can update the vector store in real time.

new_text = "Agents can be assigned to roles for specialized tasks."

vectorstore.add_texts([new_text])

This supports continual learning, allowing agents to grow more intelligent over time.

Managing Metadata

You can enrich documents with metadata (like author, topic, timestamp) and use filtering during retrieval.

docs = [

   {"text": "LangGraph supports graph-based workflows.", "metadata": {"source": "docs"}},

```
  {"text": "CrewAI supports task delegation.", "metadata":
{"source": "blog"}}

]
```

```
from langchain.schema import Document
```

```
documents = [Document(page_content=d["text"],
metadata=d["metadata"]) for d in docs]
```

```
vectorstore = FAISS.from_documents(documents,
embedding_model)
```

Later, you can filter by metadata during search if needed.

Personal Tip

When building a memory system, don't dump entire documents
into the vector store. Chunk them into smaller, meaningful
passages (e.g., 2–3 sentences) for more accurate matches. This is
especially important when agents use the memory in conversation
or reasoning tasks.

Vector stores unlock true memory capabilities for agents. By embedding knowledge, you allow them to reason over meaning rather than surface-level keywords, making interactions more natural and useful.

8.4 Long-Term Memory and Context Persistence

For agents to act intelligently across extended interactions, they need more than short-term memory. They must recall past goals, user preferences, prior conversations, or even mistakes. This is where long-term memory and context persistence come into play—key capabilities that allow agents to behave more like human collaborators.

Why Long-Term Memory Matters

Imagine an assistant that remembers what you worked on last week, knows your preferences for communication style, or tracks the progress of multi-step projects. Without persistent memory, every session starts from scratch. With it, agents can offer continuity, personalization, and depth of understanding.

Types of Memory

- **Short-Term Memory**: Limited to the current conversation or task; typically stored in a prompt.

- **Long-Term Memory**: Persistent, retrieved from databases or vector stores across sessions.

- **Contextual State**: Structured knowledge like goals, flags, or workflow state saved in code or external storage.

Techniques for Persisting Agent Context

There are several strategies you can use to give agents a sense of memory and continuity:

1. Session Logging and Replay

Store prior interactions as plain text or structured logs. When a new session starts, replay relevant segments into the context.

```
# Store conversation history in a list or database

history = [

   "User: I want to automate my market analysis",

   "Agent: Sure, we can build a multi-agent crew for that."

]
```

```
# Inject history into the agent's prompt

prompt = "\n".join(history) + "\nCurrent User: How do I analyze
competitors?"
```

This approach works well for chat-based agents and can be
enhanced with summarization if the logs grow too long.

2. Using Vector Stores for Semantic Recall

Store contextual facts or observations as vectors so the agent can
retrieve them based on meaning rather than exact phrasing.

```
# After a session

summary = "User prefers concise responses and uses GPT-4"

vectorstore.add_texts([summary])
```

```
# On new session

query = "What does the user prefer?"

results = vectorstore.similarity_search(query)
```

This enables memory access based on user questions or internal logic.

3. Persistent Metadata on Task Objects

When agents perform tasks with CrewAI or LangGraph, you can attach metadata that persists across runs.

```
task = Task(

    description="Summarize product feedback from reviews",

    metadata={"user_id": "user123", "last_run": "2024-05-01"}

)
```

This metadata can be used to determine relevance, prevent repetition, or personalize behavior.

Building a Memory Layer

Let's create a simple memory system with long-term storage using a file-based approach. This can be replaced with a database or vector store in production.

Step 1: Saving Memory

```python
import json


def save_user_memory(user_id, memory):

    with open(f"{user_id}_memory.json", "w") as f:

        json.dump(memory, f)
```

Step 2: Loading Memory

```python
def load_user_memory(user_id):

    try:

        with open(f"{user_id}_memory.json") as f:

            return json.load(f)

    except FileNotFoundError:

        return {}
```

Step 3: Using Memory in the Agent Prompt

```python
user_id = "user123"
```

```
memory = load_user_memory(user_id)

context = memory.get("preferences", "")
```

```
prompt = f"User prefers: {context}\nCurrent input: Generate a
summary"
```

You can also use this system to track task history, store last known goals, or even log emotional tone if you're working with empathetic agents.

Synchronizing with Workflow State

If you're using LangGraph or CrewAI, memory can be synced with agent state transitions.

For example, after a node completes in LangGraph, write a summary of the node's output to persistent memory. Later, this summary can be injected back into another node's input.

```
state["memory"].append({"step": "analyze_reviews", "output":
analysis})
```

Agents that read from this memory key can use the results to inform decisions downstream.

Personal Insight

A mistake I've made in earlier projects was treating memory as just more context to cram into a prompt. That doesn't scale. Real long-term memory needs selective recall—surfacing only what's relevant at the right time. That's why combining persistent storage with semantic search or structured metadata makes a huge difference.

When done right, long-term memory unlocks sophisticated behaviors: learning user style, recognizing repeated requests, refining strategies, and evolving over time.

8.5 Best Practices for Tool-Agent Interactions

As AI agents become more capable, their effectiveness increasingly depends on how well they use tools—whether it's web search, code execution, file reading, or external APIs. Good tooling can make a basic agent feel powerful. Poor tool integration, on the other hand, can lead to confusion, unnecessary retries, or even hallucinated behavior.

This section covers best practices that ensure your agents use tools effectively and reliably across LangGraph, CrewAI, or hybrid frameworks.

Match the Right Tool to the Right Agent

Every agent should be explicitly aware of the tools available to it. Give each agent a well-defined scope, and only assign tools that directly support its role.

For example:

```
research_agent = Agent(

    role="Market Research Analyst",

    tools=[GoogleSearchTool(), FileReader()],

    backstory="You specialize in gathering insights from public sources."

)
```

This avoids overloading general-purpose agents and helps enforce role specialization. Keep the agent's toolset focused, not universal.

Always Include Tool Usage Examples in Prompts

Agents often fail to use tools properly if they aren't shown how. Use a few-shot learning approach to demonstrate the correct usage pattern.

```
prompt = """
```

You are a research assistant with access to the 'search' tool.

When needed, invoke the tool like this:

```
<tool>search</tool>[query]
```


Example:

```
<tool>search</tool>Top emerging EV startups in 2025
```

```
"""
```


Even if the tool is technically available, the agent needs clear, human-readable instructions on when and how to use it.

Use Structured Input and Output Interfaces

Tools should have a predictable format. This reduces parsing errors and makes downstream chaining easier.

Example: Instead of returning raw text, structure your response.

```
class GetStockPriceTool(BaseTool):

    name = "get_stock_price"

    description = "Fetch current stock price for a given symbol"


    def run(self, symbol: str) -> dict:

        # Mocked data for simplicity

        return {

            "symbol": symbol,

            "price": 127.45,

            "currency": "USD"

        }
```

Now your agent can respond more precisely:

```
price_info = tool.run("TSLA")

response = f"TSLA is trading at {price_info['price']}
{price_info['currency']}."
```

Validate Tool Inputs Before Execution

It's common for agents to hallucinate tool arguments. Use input validators to catch errors early.

```
def run(self, symbol: str) -> dict:

    if not symbol.isalpha():

        raise ValueError("Invalid stock symbol format.")
```

You can also add a fallback message if validation fails:

```
try:

    result = tool.run(input)

except Exception:

    result = {"error": "Invalid input provided to the tool."}
```

Rate-Limit and Retry Intelligently

When working with external APIs or costly tools (like code execution), use backoff strategies and retry logic.

```python
import time

from requests.exceptions import RequestException


def safe_tool_call(fn, retries=3):
    for i in range(retries):
        try:
            return fn()
        except RequestException:
            time.sleep(2 ** i)
    return {"error": "Tool failed after multiple attempts."}
```

Wrap tool calls in this handler to reduce unexpected failures.

Log Tool Usage for Transparency

Tracking which tools agents used, with what inputs and outputs, helps with debugging and improvement.

```
log_entry = {

    "tool": "search",

    "input": "EV startups in 2025",

    "output": search_results

}

save_log(log_entry)
```

Logging is especially important in production environments where tracing behavior is critical.

Avoid Overuse of Tools in a Single Pass

Some agents go tool-crazy if not prompted properly. You can limit tool usage with token guards or prompt-based reminders.

```
prompt += "\nOnly use tools if absolutely necessary. Aim to respond concisely."
```

Or track tool usage count per run:

```
if tool_usage_count > 2:

    skip_tool_invocation()
```

This keeps the response efficient and prevents looping.

Personal Insight

Early in my experiments, I gave agents too many tools—search, browser, calculator, API runner, file reader—all at once. The result? They rarely used any of them correctly. Once I started pruning tools to only those essential for their task and including examples, tool usage shot up in accuracy and relevance. Simplicity and clarity beat abundance every time.

Summary

Here's a checklist of best practices:

- Scope each agent's tools to its specific role

- Provide examples of how and when to use tools

- Enforce structured input/output schemas

- Validate tool inputs and handle errors gracefully

- Use retry logic and backoff for external services

- Log all tool interactions for visibility

- Cap excessive tool usage per session

Mastering tool-agent interactions is essential for building robust, reliable AI workflows. As your agents take on more sophisticated tasks, strong tooling is what lets them act with precision and purpose.

Chapter 9: Deployment and Production Readiness

Shipping AI agent workflows from notebooks to production environments is a critical step that determines their real-world reliability and usefulness. This chapter guides you through the essential practices and strategies for deploying LangGraph and CrewAI-based applications. We'll cover everything from wrapping workflows with APIs, containerization, and automation, to monitoring, cost management, and handling operational challenges.

9.1 From Notebook to Production

Many AI agent workflows begin life in a Jupyter Notebook. It's the ideal playground—flexible, visual, and interactive. But notebooks aren't built for reliability, collaboration, or automation. Transitioning from exploratory development to a robust production system means embracing a different mindset, structure, and toolset.

Why Moving to Production Matters

Notebooks are great for experimentation, but production demands:

- Reusability: Code should be modular and testable

- Reliability: Systems need consistent behavior under various conditions

- Deployability: Your application should be containerized, scalable, and ready for CI/CD

To move your LangGraph or CrewAI project from notebook to production, you'll need to refactor, modularize, and integrate it into a standard Python project structure.

Step 1: Refactor Your Notebook Code

Start by identifying reusable components in your notebook—agents, tools, workflows—and move them into Python modules.

Example folder structure:

my_agent_project/

├── agents/

│   └── researcher.py

├── tools/

```
|      └── web_search.py
├── workflows/
|      └── summarize_pipeline.py
├── app.py
├── requirements.txt
└── README.md
```

Each module should encapsulate a single responsibility. For instance, your researcher.py file might contain:

```python
from crewai import Agent, Task


def create_research_agent():
    return Agent(
        role="Researcher",
        goal="Find and extract accurate information from reliable sources",
```

```
    backstory="An academic researcher with expertise in data
analysis"

    )
```

This makes your logic testable, debuggable, and much easier to
maintain.

Step 2: Externalize Configuration

Avoid hardcoding API keys, model parameters, or
environment-specific values. Use .env files and the python-dotenv
library to load environment variables securely:

```
# .env

OPENAI_API_KEY=your-key-here


# config.py

from dotenv import load_dotenv

import os


load_dotenv()
```

```
OPENAI_API_KEY = os.getenv("OPENAI_API_KEY")
```

This improves portability and security.

Step 3: Add Logging

Print statements don't cut it in production. Use Python's logging module to track behavior and errors in a structured way.

```
import logging
```

```
logging.basicConfig(level=logging.INFO)
```

```
logger = logging.getLogger(__name__)
```

```
logger.info("Agent initialized")
```

You can later redirect logs to external systems like Sentry, DataDog, or CloudWatch for better observability.

Step 4: Write Tests

Test the components of your system independently using pytest or unittest.

```python
def test_create_research_agent():

    agent = create_research_agent()

    assert agent.role == "Researcher"
```

This helps catch regressions early as you iterate and scale.

Step 5: Create an Entry Point

Build a CLI or API to trigger workflows outside the notebook. For starters, a simple CLI with argparse can work:

```python
import argparse

from workflows.summarize_pipeline import run_workflow


if __name__ == "__main__":

    parser = argparse.ArgumentParser()

    parser.add_argument("query", help="Search query for the research pipeline")
```

```
args = parser.parse_args()



run_workflow(args.query)
```

This makes your pipeline executable from a terminal or cron job.

Step 6: Prepare for Deployment

Once modularized and tested, wrap your app for deployment. This typically includes:

- Creating a Dockerfile

- Setting up version control with Git

- Integrating with CI/CD pipelines

- Hosting APIs with FastAPI or Flask (covered in Section 9.2)

Basic Dockerfile:

```
FROM python:3.10
```

```
WORKDIR /app


COPY . .


RUN pip install -r requirements.txt


CMD ["python", "app.py"]
```

You can now build and run the container:

```
docker build -t ai-agent-app .

docker run --env-file .env ai-agent-app
```


Personal Insight

One of the most common issues I've seen when helping teams
productionize AI workflows is letting notebooks grow too large
before modularizing. It's tempting to wait until things "settle,"
but you'll end up with a spaghetti mess that's hard to untangle.
Refactor early—even if the final structure changes later.

Summary Checklist

- Move code from notebook into modules

- Externalize all configuration

- Add proper logging

- Write unit tests

- Create a CLI or API entry point

- Package and containerize

This foundational work sets the stage for production deployment, scalability, and monitoring. In the next section, we'll cover how to expose your workflow via API and Dockerize it for deployment.

9.2 Wrapping Workflows with FastAPI & Docker

Once your AI agent workflow is modularized and testable, the next step is to make it accessible—whether to a front-end application, a scheduled job, or another system. FastAPI is an excellent choice for this. It's fast, intuitive, and designed with modern Python features like type hints and async support. Paired with Docker, it gives you a reproducible environment that's easy to deploy anywhere.

Why Use FastAPI?

FastAPI lets you expose your AI agent as a web service with minimal overhead. It comes with automatic docs via Swagger and supports async operations—perfect for agent-based workflows that might involve I/O, such as web scraping or API calls.

Step 1: Create a FastAPI App

Assume you already have a LangGraph or CrewAI workflow defined in a function like run_workflow(query).

Start by setting up your FastAPI app in a file like main.py.

```python
from fastapi import FastAPI, HTTPException

from pedantic import BaseModel

from workflows.summarize_pipeline import run_workflow


app = FastAPI()


class RequestBody(BaseModel):
    query: str
```

```python
@app.post("/run")

def run_agent(request: RequestBody):

    try:

        result = run_workflow(request.query)

        return {"result": result}

    except Exception as e:

        raise HTTPException(status_code=500, detail=str(e))
```

With just a few lines, you now have an endpoint that will accept a POST request and return the agent's output.

To run this locally:

```
uvicorn main:app --reload
```

Navigate to http://127.0.0.1:8000/docs and you'll see an interactive API UI.

Step 2: Structure for Deployment

Make sure your project structure is clean:

```
ai_service/
├── agents/
├── tools/
├── workflows/
├── main.py
├── requirements.txt
└── Dockerfile
```

requirements.txt

fastapi

uvicorn

crewai

openai

python-dotenv

Adjust packages as needed depending on your workflow.

Step 3: Add Docker Support

Now it's time to containerize your FastAPI app so it can be deployed to the cloud, integrated with orchestration tools, or run reliably on any server.

Dockerfile

FROM python:3.10

WORKDIR /app

COPY . .

RUN pip install --no-cache-dir -r requirements.txt

CMD ["uvicorn", "main:app", "--host", "0.0.0.0", "--port", "8000"]

.dockerignore

__pycache__/

```
*.pyc
```

```
.env
```

Build and run the Docker container:

```
docker build -t ai-agent-api .
```

```
docker run -p 8000:8000 --env-file .env ai-agent-api
```

You now have a containerized API that can be deployed on a cloud VM, Kubernetes cluster, or even serverless container service like AWS Fargate.

Step 4: Environment Management

Use a .env file to store sensitive credentials and model keys:

```
OPENAI_API_KEY=your-key
```

Load them in your code using python-dotenv:

```
from dotenv import load_dotenv
```

```
import os
```

```python
load_dotenv()

OPENAI_API_KEY = os.getenv("OPENAI_API_KEY")
```

Never hardcode secrets or credentials—especially when containerizing.

Step 5: Test It

Use a tool like httpie or Postman to test the API:

```
http POST http://localhost:8000/run query="Summarize OpenAI's latest news"
```

Expect a JSON response like:

```json
{

  "result": "OpenAI recently released..."

}
```

You can also hook this API up to your frontend, a Slack bot, or a scheduled automation tool.

Pro Tip: Use Async When Possible

If your agent performs a lot of I/O (e.g., calling APIs or scraping web pages), consider making your run_workflow() function asynchronous. FastAPI supports this natively and it will improve performance under load.

Personal Insight

I've seen teams spend days troubleshooting slow Flask apps, only to switch to FastAPI and get an instant performance boost with less code. It's also easier to onboard teammates thanks to the auto-generated Swagger docs.

Recap

- FastAPI makes it easy to expose your workflow as an API

- Docker ensures consistent, reproducible deployments

- Use .env files for secure configuration

- Always modularize your workflow logic before wrapping it with a web server

With your workflow now accessible over HTTP, you're ready to schedule it, monitor it, or plug it into a broader production system—which we'll tackle in the next section.

9.3 Scheduling and Automation with Cron, n8n, or Airflow

Once your AI agent workflows are packaged and available via an API or CLI command, the next step is making them run without manual input. Whether you're collecting daily market insights, automating report generation, or monitoring user feedback, scheduling and automation turn reactive tools into proactive services.

There are several ways to automate your workflows depending on your complexity needs. Here's a breakdown of three popular options: **Cron, n8n**, and **Apache Airflow**—along with when to use each.

Using Cron for Simple Scheduling

Best for: Lightweight, local or server-based jobs that don't need detailed orchestration.

If you've got a Dockerized API or a Python script that should run on a schedule (like every hour or once a day), Cron is a dependable tool that's been around forever.

Step 1: Create a Python CLI Script

Let's say your agent is exposed via a function run_workflow() in a script:

```
# file: agent_runner.py

from workflows.daily_news import run_workflow


if __name__ == "__main__":

    result = run_workflow()

    print(result)
```

Step 2: Create a Cron Job

Edit your crontab with:

```
crontab -e
```

Then add an entry to run the script every day at 8 AM:

```
0 8 * * * /usr/bin/python3 /path/to/agent_runner.py >>
/path/to/logs/agent.log 2>&1
```

Tips:

- Make sure the Python environment has all dependencies installed.

- Redirect logs so you can debug failures later.

Using n8n for Low-Code Automation

Best for: Connecting your agent to webhooks, APIs, email, Google Sheets, Slack, etc., with minimal code.

n8n (pronounced "n-eight-n") is a low-code automation tool that runs in your browser and gives you a visual workflow builder—great for integrating agents with other services.

Step 1: Install n8n

```
npm install n8n -g
```

```
n8n start
```

You can also run it with Docker:

```
docker run -it --rm -p 5678:5678 n8nio/n8n
```

Step 2: Build a Workflow

1. Create a **Cron Trigger** node.

2. Add an **HTTP Request** node to call your FastAPI or Flask endpoint.

3. Optionally, chain a Slack or Gmail node to send the agent's response somewhere useful.

Benefits:

- No need to write orchestration logic.

- Built-in retry and failure tracking.

- Easy webhook-to-agent pipelines.

Example: You can trigger an AI research assistant every Monday at 9 AM, collect summaries from multiple news sources, and auto-send an email digest.

Using Apache Airflow for Complex Pipelines

Best for: Enterprise-grade task management, dependencies, retries, parallelism, and detailed monitoring.

Airflow is a robust scheduler and workflow manager built for data engineering. It works great for agents that are part of larger pipelines.

Step 1: Define a DAG

Here's a simple Airflow DAG that runs your agent:

```
# file: dags/agent_dag.py

from airflow import DAG

from airflow.operators.python_operator import PythonOperator

from datetime import datetime, timedelta

from workflows.daily_report import run_workflow


default_args = {
```

```python
    "owner": "airflow",

    "retries": 1,

    "retry_delay": timedelta(minutes=5),

}


with DAG(

    "ai_agent_workflow",

    start_date=datetime(2024, 1, 1),

    schedule_interval="@daily",

    catchup=False,

    default_args=default_args,

    tags=["ai", "agent"],

) as dag:


    run_agent = PythonOperator(

        task_id="run_ai_agent",
```

```
python_callable=run_workflow,

)
```

Step 2: Start Airflow

```
airflow db init

airflow users create --username admin --password admin --role
Admin --email admin@example.com

airflow webserver --port 8080

airflow scheduler
```

Visit http://localhost:8080 to manage and monitor jobs.

Why Use Airflow?

- Retry failed jobs with backoff policies.

- Chain tasks with conditional logic.

- Track executions in detail via a UI.

Summary: Choosing the Right Tool

Tool	Best For	Complexity	Strengths
Cron	Simple recurring jobs	Low	Lightweight, no dependencies
n8n	API integrations & no-code UI	Medium	Easy to connect services
Airflow	Data pipelines & orchestration	High	Full monitoring, dependencies, retries

Personal Insight

For my personal agent automations—like scraping updates and pushing summaries to Notion—n8n is a lifesaver. I use Cron on edge devices and fallback jobs. When building with a team or chaining multiple data-processing agents, Airflow is a no-brainer.

9.4 Monitoring, Logging, and Error Handling

Once your agents are in production, the game shifts from building to maintaining. Monitoring, logging, and error handling aren't optional—they're essential. Even a simple oversight like a silent failure or a malformed response can throw off an entire automation pipeline or confuse end users. This section walks you through how to set up these systems properly, and more importantly, how to use them to keep things running smoothly.

Monitoring: Know When Something Breaks (or Works)

Monitoring helps you detect anomalies, track performance, and get alerted before users start complaining. You can use lightweight solutions like Prometheus + Grafana for metrics, or more robust platforms like Datadog, New Relic, or AWS CloudWatch.

Step 1: Expose Agent Health and Metrics

If you're using FastAPI, expose a health check route and collect basic metrics:

```python
from fastapi import FastAPI

from prometheus_client import Counter, generate_latest


app = FastAPI()


agent_calls = Counter("agent_calls_total", "Total agent calls")

agent_failures = Counter("agent_failures_total", "Total agent failures")


@app.get("/health")

def health():

    return {"status": "ok"}


@app.get("/metrics")

def metrics():

    return Response(generate_latest(), media_type="text/plain")
```

```python
@app.post("/run-agent")

def run_agent():

    try:

        agent_calls.inc()

        # run your agent logic

        return {"result": "success"}

    except Exception:

        agent_failures.inc()

        raise
```

Use a Prometheus server to scrape /metrics, and hook it into Grafana for alerts like "failures > 5 in 10 minutes."

Logging: The Trail of Truth

Logging is your time machine. It helps you debug issues that happened yesterday—or last month. You'll want logs that are:

- Structured (JSON preferred)

- Centralized (e.g., sent to Logstash, FluentBit, or a cloud logger)

- Level-based (info, warning, error)

Step 1: Use Python's Logging Module with JSON

```python
import logging

import json_log_formatter


formatter = json_log_formatter.JSONFormatter()


handler = logging.FileHandler(filename="/var/log/agent.log")

handler.setFormatter(formatter)


logger = logging.getLogger("agent_logger")

logger.addHandler(handler)
```

```
logger.setLevel(logging.INFO)


logger.info("Agent started", extra={"agent": "market-analyzer",
"status": "init"})
```

Step 2: Log Key Execution Milestones

Within your agent:

```
try:

    logger.info("Fetching data", extra={"step": "fetch"})

    # fetch logic

    logger.info("Generating insights", extra={"step": "process"})

    # processing logic

except Exception as e:

    logger.error("Agent failed", extra={"error": str(e)})
```

If you're containerized, mount logs to stdout/stderr and aggregate with a tool like Loki, ELK, or AWS CloudWatch Logs.

Error Handling: Catch, Recover, Retry

Agents will fail. APIs change. Models time out. Network issues happen. Your job is to make failure graceful, detectable, and recoverable.

Step 1: Use Try/Except Around Core Logic

```
def run_workflow():

    try:

        data = fetch_data()

    except TimeoutError:

        logger.warning("Timeout while fetching data", extra={"retry": True})

        data = fetch_data(retry=True)


    try:

        result = analyze_data(data)

    except Exception as e:
```

```python
        logger.error("Analysis failed", extra={"error": str(e)})

        notify_admin(str(e))

        raise
```

Step 2: Use Circuit Breakers and Retries

For network-based tasks (APIs, tools), use tenacity to auto-retry:

```python
from tenacity import retry, wait_fixed, stop_after_attempt


@retry(wait=wait_fixed(2), stop=stop_after_attempt(3))
def call_tool():
    return external_api_call()
```

Step 3: Notify When Things Go Wrong

Automated alerts can be sent to Slack, PagerDuty, or even email:

```python
def notify_admin(error_message):
    requests.post("https://hooks.slack.com/...", json={
```

```
    "text": f"Agent failed: {error_message}"

})
```

Practical Setup Checklist

- Log everything meaningful (but not excessively)

- Use structured logs and rotate them

- Expose metrics (requests, failures, latencies)

- Add retry mechanisms for flaky tasks

- Set up alerts on failure patterns

- Have graceful fallbacks and notification channels

Personal Insight

I once deployed an autonomous newsletter generator that silently failed for three weeks because I'd forgotten to connect logs to my dashboard. The lesson? Assume things will break and make it impossible not to notice. A single error email or Slack ping would've saved hours of debugging.

Solid monitoring and logging are like insurance policies for your agents. They don't just help you fix problems—they help you trust your system enough to let it run without constant babysitting. In the next section, we'll tackle how to manage API tokens, cost constraints, and model reliability in a production environment.

9.5 Managing Tokens, Cost, and API Reliability

Large Language Models don't come cheap, especially when you're chaining multiple API calls inside a multi-agent workflow. Token usage, cost, and API stability can sneak up and break your system—or your budget. This section shows you how to gain visibility into what's happening under the hood and how to stay in control of expenses and reliability.

Understanding Token Costs and Budget Control

Every API call to a model like OpenAI, Anthropic, or Mistral costs money, usually tied to the number of tokens processed in the prompt and response. You need to monitor:

- **Total token usage**

- **Tokens per agent interaction**

- **Prompt vs. completion ratio**

- **Per-run and per-day usage trends**

Step 1: Enable Token Counting

If you're using OpenAI via LangChain or directly, wrap the call with a token logger:

import tik tok

```
def count_tokens(prompt, model="gpt-4"):

  enc = tiktoken.encoding_for_model(model)

  return len(enc.encode(prompt))
```

```
prompt = "Analyze this report and summarize key risks..."

response = openai.ChatCompletion.create(

  model="gpt-4",
```

```python
    messages=[{"role": "user", "content": prompt}]
)


input_tokens = count_tokens(prompt)

output_tokens =
count_tokens(response['choices'][0]['message']['content'])

print(f"Tokens used: {input_tokens + output_tokens}")
```

Use this to track how much each agent is costing per run.

Step 2: Set Soft Token Limits

Implement usage guards in your pipeline:

```python
MAX_TOKENS_PER_RUN = 4000


if input_tokens + output_tokens >
MAX_TOKENS_PER_RUN:

    raise Exception("Token budget exceeded for this run")
```

You can also cap daily usage by aggregating token logs and checking before each run.

Controlling Cost with Model Tiering

Different models cost different amounts. GPT-4 is powerful but expensive. GPT-3.5 or Claude Instant may be sufficient for simpler tasks.

Strategy: Assign cheaper models to less critical tasks

```
if task_type == "summarization":

    use_model("gpt-3.5-turbo")

elif task_type == "decision_making":

    use_model("gpt-4")
```

LangChain and CrewAI support per-agent model config, so you can easily do this at the agent level.

API Reliability and Failover Handling

API downtime, rate limits, and slow responses can be deal-breakers in production. Protect your workflows with:

- Retry mechanisms

- Fallback models

- Timeouts

- Rate limiting

Step 1: Add Retry Logic with Backoff

from tenacity import retry, wait_exponential, stop_after_attempt

```
@retry(wait=wait_exponential(multiplier=1, min=2, max=10),
stop=stop_after_attempt(3))
def call_model(prompt):
  return openai.ChatCompletion.create(
    model="gpt-4",
    messages=[{"role": "user", "content": prompt}],
    timeout=10
  )
```

Step 2: Fallback to Alternate Provider or Model

```
try:

  response = call_model(prompt)

except Exception:

  response = anthropic.Completion.create(

    model="claude-instant-1",

    prompt=prompt,

    stop_sequences=["\n\n"],

    max_tokens_to_sample=300

  )
```

Step 3: Use a Proxy or Rate-Limiting Layer

To avoid rate-limit errors, queue requests or use a proxy like OpenRouter or LangChain's Router module to distribute calls:

```
from langchain.chat_models import ChatOpenAI, ChatAnthropic
```

```
router = Router([

   {"model": ChatOpenAI(model="gpt-3.5-turbo"), "weight": 70},

   {"model": ChatAnthropic(model="claude-instant-1"), "weight":
30}

])
```

response = router.call(prompt)

This ensures you're not overloading one endpoint while leaving others idle.

Budget Reporting and Alerting

Automated reporting helps you track usage trends and stay within budget.

Step 1: Log Token Usage to a CSV or Database

import csv

from datetime import datetime

```python
def log_usage(agent, tokens):

    with open("usage_log.csv", "a") as f:

        writer = csv.writer(f)

        writer.writerow([datetime.utcnow(), agent, tokens])
```

Step 2: Set Budget Thresholds and Alerts

Aggregate logs daily, and trigger alerts if usage spikes unexpectedly. You can use a Python script or external dashboard like Metabase or Grafana.

```python
if daily_total_tokens > DAILY_LIMIT:

    send_slack_alert(f"Token usage high: {daily_total_tokens} tokens today")
```

Tips for Staying Efficient

- Use embeddings for context instead of long prompts

- Store static knowledge in vector stores to avoid redundant LLM calls

- Prune chat histories aggressively to avoid token bloating

- Prefer summarization over full transcripts when chaining tasks

- Avoid calling models to do tasks that deterministic code can handle (e.g., formatting)

Personal Insight

When running a multi-agent project in production, I noticed that a single agent—responsible for wrapping up results—used over 60% of the total token budget due to verbose summary formatting. Swapping it with a templated prompt and post-processing logic cut the cost in half without sacrificing quality. The lesson? Audit your agents. Some are quietly expensive.

Managing cost, token usage, and reliability isn't just about saving money—it's about building systems that scale confidently. The best setups monitor themselves, optimize usage automatically, and gracefully degrade when services hiccup. These are the systems you can trust to run unattended, even at scale.

Chapter 10: Real-World Projects

Chapter 10 focuses on bringing all the concepts together by showcasing complete, production-ready multi-agent workflows. These real-world examples demonstrate how to build end-to-end systems using LangGraph, CrewAI, or both. Each project addresses a practical use case with the goal of inspiring readers to experiment with or extend the designs based on their needs.

10.1 AI Research Assistant

Building an AI-powered research assistant is a great way to combine LangGraph's flow control with CrewAI's human-like delegation. The goal is to automate the gathering, summarizing, cross-referencing, and reporting of research content from online and offline sources.

Defining the Use Case

Let's say we want an assistant that takes a research query, finds credible sources, extracts key insights, summarizes them, and provides proper citations. This is especially helpful for content creators, analysts, and knowledge workers.

Step 1: Setting Up the Agent Framework

We start by defining three core agents using CrewAI:

```python
from crewai import Agent, Task, Crew

from langchain.tools import DuckDuckGoSearchRun


search_tool = DuckDuckGoSearchRun()


researcher = Agent(

    role="Researcher",

    goal="Find credible information from the web and summarize findings",

    backstory="An expert in information gathering and critical analysis",

    tools=[search_tool],

    verbose=True

)


summarizer = Agent(
```

```
    role="Summarizer",

    goal="Read findings and write concise summaries with
citations",

    backstory="Skilled in condensing detailed texts into digestible
insights",

    verbose=True

)


writer = Agent(

    role="Writer",

    goal="Compile summarized findings into a structured, readable
report",

    backstory="Experienced technical writer with attention to
clarity and structure",

    verbose=True

)
```

Step 2: Task Definition and Flow

We'll define three sequential tasks, each building on the previous:

```
research_task = Task(

    description="Search the web for relevant and credible sources
    about the impact of AI on remote work.",

    agent=researcher

)



summary_task = Task(

    description="Summarize the content found by the Researcher
    into key points with proper citations.",

    agent=summarizer

)



writeup_task = Task(

    description="Create a structured research summary report
    based on the Summarizer's findings.",

    agent=writer
```

```
)


crew = Crew(

    agents=[researcher, summarizer, writer],

    tasks=[research_task, summary_task, writeup_task],

    verbose=True

)



output = crew.kickoff()

print(output)
```

Step 3: Optional LangGraph Integration

LangGraph can help manage dynamic state transitions—like branching based on the confidence level of sources. Here's how a basic controller might look:

```
import langgraph
```

```
@langgraph.node

async def validate_sources(state):

    if state['source_quality'] < 0.7:

        return {"next": "re_research"}

    return {"next": "summarize"}


# Combine with CrewAI logic or tasks inside LangGraph
```

Personal Insight

I've found that using multiple specialized agents with defined roles greatly improves output quality. It mimics how actual research teams operate: gather, condense, write. Integrating retrieval tools like DuckDuckGo or SerpAPI and memory tools like a vector store can elevate the assistant from simple automation to a knowledge-aware assistant.

Deployment Suggestions

- Wrap the Crew in a FastAPI endpoint

- Store responses in a database like Supabase or Firestore

- Schedule runs with n8n or Airflow for recurring topics

This assistant can be scaled across domains—tech, health, education—by changing prompts and tuning agent personalities. It's one of the most useful patterns to prototype real-world agent workflows.

10.1 AI Research Assistant

Building an AI-powered research assistant is a great way to combine LangGraph's flow control with CrewAI's human-like delegation. The goal is to automate the gathering, summarizing, cross-referencing, and reporting of research content from online and offline sources.

Defining the Use Case

Let's say we want an assistant that takes a research query, finds credible sources, extracts key insights, summarizes them, and provides proper citations. This is especially helpful for content creators, analysts, and knowledge workers.

Step 1: Setting Up the Agent Framework

We start by defining three core agents using CrewAI:

```python
from crewai import Agent, Task, Crew

from langchain.tools import DuckDuckGoSearchRun


search_tool = DuckDuckGoSearchRun()


researcher = Agent(

    role="Researcher",

    goal="Find credible information from the web and summarize findings",

    backstory="An expert in information gathering and critical analysis",

    tools=[search_tool],

    verbose=True

)


summarizer = Agent(

    role="Summarizer",
```

```
    goal="Read findings and write concise summaries with
citations",

    backstory="Skilled in condensing detailed texts into digestible
insights",

    verbose=True

)


writer = Agent(

    role="Writer",

    goal="Compile summarized findings into a structured, readable
report",

    backstory="Experienced technical writer with attention to
clarity and structure",

    verbose=True

)
```

Step 2: Task Definition and Flow

We'll define three sequential tasks, each building on the previous:

```
research_task = Task(

    description="Search the web for relevant and credible sources
    about the impact of AI on remote work.",

    agent=researcher

)


summary_task = Task(

    description="Summarize the content found by the Researcher
    into key points with proper citations.",

    agent=summarizer

)


writeup_task = Task(

    description="Create a structured research summary report
    based on the Summarizer's findings.",

    agent=writer

)
```

```
crew = Crew(

    agents=[researcher, summarizer, writer],

    tasks=[research_task, summary_task, writeup_task],

    verbose=True

)


output = crew.kickoff()

print(output)
```

Step 3: Optional LangGraph Integration

LangGraph can help manage dynamic state transitions—like branching based on the confidence level of sources. Here's how a basic controller might look:

```
import langgraph


@langgraph.node
```

```python
async def validate_sources(state):

    if state['source_quality'] < 0.7:

        return {"next": "re_research"}

    return {"next": "summarize"}



# Combine with CrewAI logic or tasks inside LangGraph
```

Personal Insight

I've found that using multiple specialized agents with defined roles greatly improves output quality. It mimics how actual research teams operate: gather, condense, write. Integrating retrieval tools like DuckDuckGo or SerpAPI and memory tools like a vector store can elevate the assistant from simple automation to a knowledge-aware assistant.

Deployment Suggestions

- Wrap the Crew in a FastAPI endpoint

- Store responses in a database like Supabase or Firestore

- Schedule runs with n8n or Airflow for recurring topics

This assistant can be scaled across domains—tech, health, education—by changing prompts and tuning agent personalities. It's one of the most useful patterns to prototype real-world agent workflows.

10.2 Business Intelligence Reporter

A Business Intelligence (BI) Reporter powered by LangGraph and CrewAI can automate the collection, analysis, and reporting of market and internal data for strategic decision-making. This type of agent workflow is invaluable for companies looking to gain data-driven insights without constantly relying on manual reporting.

Defining the Use Case

Imagine you want to automate a weekly BI report that summarizes sales performance, customer sentiment, and competitor activities. The system needs to pull structured data from databases and APIs, run custom analytics, and format the results into a presentation or executive summary.

Step 1: Define Agents and Tools

Let's build a team of agents specialized in data sourcing, analysis, and reporting:

```python
from crewai import Agent, Task, Crew

from langchain.tools import Tool


class SQLQueryTool:

    def __call__(self, query):

        # Connect to database and return result

        return execute_query(query)


data_tool = SQLQueryTool()


analyst = Agent(

    role="Data Analyst",

    goal="Run data queries and compute metrics for business insights",

    backstory="An experienced analyst fluent in SQL and data trends",

    tools=[data_tool],
```

```python
    verbose=True

)


insight_agent = Agent(

    role="Insight Generator",

    goal="Interpret analysis results and detect key trends or
anomalies",

    backstory="Expert in interpreting metrics and identifying
insights",

    verbose=True

)


reporter = Agent(

    role="Reporter",

    goal="Create clear, concise reports summarizing findings",

    backstory="Professional BI writer skilled in executive
communication",
```

```
    verbose=True

)
```

Step 2: Create the Workflow

The sequence of tasks should reflect the analysis lifecycle:

```
query_task = Task(

    description="Fetch sales, churn, and web traffic data for the past
30 days.",

    agent=analyst

)



insight_task = Task(

    description="Analyze the data and generate key insights and
trends.",

    agent=insight_agent

)
```

```
report_task = Task(

    description="Write a business intelligence summary
    highlighting key findings.",

    agent=reporter

)


crew = Crew(

    agents=[analyst, insight_agent, reporter],

    tasks=[query_task, insight_task, report_task],

    verbose=True

)


result = crew.kickoff()

print(result)
```

Step 3: Enhancing with LangGraph

LangGraph can introduce dynamic flow control. For example, if anomalies are found, you can route to a root-cause analysis node before proceeding to report:

import langgraph

@langgraph.node

async def check_for_anomalies(state):

   if state.get("anomaly_detected"):

     return {"next": "root_cause_analysis"}

     return {"next": "generate_report"}

Deployment Ideas

- Schedule this agent to run weekly using Airflow or n8n

- Store raw data snapshots and generated reports in a document store

- Use a vector database for memory if historical insights should influence interpretation

Personal Insight

This type of automation frees analysts from repetitive tasks and gives decision-makers up-to-date insights without delay. You can scale it across departments—marketing, ops, finance—by reusing the same structure but customizing the queries and interpretation logic.

10.3 Autonomous Customer Support Agent

An autonomous customer support agent can significantly reduce response times and scale support operations with minimal human involvement. Combining LangGraph's state-driven orchestration with CrewAI's role-based agent system allows you to build flexible, intelligent customer service workflows that respond to user inquiries, troubleshoot issues, and escalate complex problems when necessary.

Use Case Overview

The idea is to create a support agent that handles incoming user queries, checks for known issues, provides solutions from a knowledge base, and escalates tickets to human staff if needed. It can work as a chatbot, backend microservice, or API-integrated module.

Step 1: Define Support Roles with CrewAI

We'll start with three core agents:

```python
from crewai import Agent, Task, Crew


support_bot = Agent(

    role="SupportBot",

    goal="Resolve user issues by querying the knowledge base and offering solutions",

    backstory="A friendly and responsive support assistant with access to company knowledge and FAQs",

    verbose=True

)


ticket_escalator = Agent(

    role="Escalator",

    goal="Identify unresolved issues and escalate to human support team",

    backstory="Responsible for forwarding complex or unsolved tickets with relevant context",
```

```
    verbose=True

)
```

```
feedback_collector = Agent(

    role="FeedbackCollector",

    goal="Collect feedback after resolution and update internal
logs",

    backstory="Focused on continuous improvement through user
insights",

    verbose=True

)
```

Step 2: Define the Task Workflow

These tasks follow the common customer support pattern:

```
support_task = Task(

    description="Analyze the user issue and provide a solution
from the knowledge base.",
```

```python
    agent=support_bot
)


escalation_task = Task(

    description="Check if the issue was resolved. If not, escalate it with proper details.",

    agent=ticket_escalator
)


feedback_task = Task(

    description="Ask the user for feedback and record it in the system.",

    agent=feedback_collector
)


crew = Crew(

    agents=[support_bot, ticket_escalator, feedback_collector],
```

```
    tasks=[support_task, escalation_task, feedback_task],

    verbose=True

)


response = crew.kickoff()

print(response)
```

Step 3: Add LangGraph for Conditional Flows

LangGraph is ideal for implementing conditional logic—like whether an issue was resolved. Here's a simple node to handle branching:

```
from langgraph.graph import StateGraph, node


@node

def resolve_issue(state):

    # Simulated condition

    if state.get("resolved", False):
```

```
return {"next": "feedback"}

return {"next": "escalate"}
```

You can integrate this into a StateGraph to control transitions across resolution, escalation, and feedback.

Step 4: Deploy the Agent

To make this system production-ready:

- Wrap it with a FastAPI endpoint

- Containerize with Docker

- Use a Redis or PostgreSQL backend to store session and tick
- et data

- Set up webhook listeners for chat platforms like Slack, Intercom, or WhatsApp

Personal Insight

One of the key advantages of CrewAI in this setup is its natural fit for modeling human-like workflows. By explicitly defining escalation paths and roles, the system mirrors a real support desk—minus the bottlenecks. LangGraph adds safety and reliability by guiding transitions based on defined conditions rather than hoping a model interprets a prompt correctly.

Extensions

- Integrate with vector databases like Weaviate to retrieve past support logs

- Use a tool-enabled agent with API access to fetch user order history or account status

- Add multilingual support by connecting to translation APIs

Autonomous support agents aren't just about automation—they're about creating systems that understand, adapt, and improve with each interaction. With LangGraph and CrewAI, that vision is within reach.

10.4 AI Project Manager with Delegation

An AI project manager capable of intelligent delegation is a powerful example of multi-agent collaboration. This setup handles planning, task assignment, and progress tracking—offloading the bulk of coordination work from humans to agents.

Defining the Use Case

Imagine you're running a small team building a product. Instead of manually tracking progress, assigning tasks, and following up on deliverables, an AI manager could perform those duties automatically. It would delegate tasks to specialized agents based on capabilities, monitor execution, and adapt plans when things change.

Step 1: Define Core Roles

Start by defining agents using CrewAI that match the roles typically found in a product team:

```
from crewai import Agent


planner = Agent(

    role="Project Planner",

    goal="Break down goals into structured milestones and tasks",

    backstory="An expert in task decomposition and deadline estimation",
```

```python
    verbose=True

)


delegator = Agent(

    role="Task Delegator",

    goal="Assign tasks to team members based on skills and
availability",

    backstory="Specializes in matching tasks to the right resources",

    verbose=True

)


tracker = Agent(

    role="Progress Tracker",

    goal="Monitor task progress and raise alerts for blockers",

    backstory="Keeps an eye on project status and reports
deviations",

    verbose=True
```

)

Step 2: Structure the Flow with LangGraph

LangGraph is ideal for managing project states and reacting to progress updates.

```
from langgraph.graph import StateGraph, node
```

```
@node
def plan_tasks(state):
    state['tasks'] = ["Set up frontend repo", "Design database schema", "Create API endpoints"]
    return {"next": "delegate_tasks", **state}
```

```
@node
def delegate_tasks(state):
    assignments = {task: "developer_1" for task in state['tasks']}
    state['assignments'] = assignments
```

```python
        return {"next": "track_progress", **state}


@node

def track_progress(state):

    completed = ["Set up frontend repo"]

    remaining = [t for t in state['tasks'] if t not in completed]

    state['completed'] = completed

    state['remaining'] = remaining

    return {"next": "done" if not remaining else "track_progress",
**state}


graph = StateGraph()

graph.add_node("plan_tasks", plan_tasks)

graph.add_node("delegate_tasks", delegate_tasks)

graph.add_node("track_progress", track_progress)

graph.set_entry_node("plan_tasks")
```

```
graph.set_finish_node("track_progress")

graph.compile()
```

Step 3: Add Realistic Task Inputs

To increase realism, hook your agents into your ticketing system (like Jira or Linear), calendar APIs for scheduling, and Slack or email for updates. You can replace mock task arrays with API-pulled tasks or form inputs from a dashboard.

Personal Insight

From my experience running agile teams, planning and task delegation is where most delays and miscommunication originate. AI agents trained on your project's structure and documentation can mitigate this by automating repetitive coordination, surfacing blockers, and ensuring progress doesn't stall when someone is unavailable.

Deployment Tips

- Add long-term memory with a vector store to track task history and avoid duplicate work

- Expose the AI manager via a dashboard using FastAPI + Streamlit

- Use a cron job or Airflow DAG to trigger status checks every few hours

This pattern becomes more valuable as project complexity increases. With the right setup, it transforms the AI from a passive assistant to an active project orchestrator.

10.5 Workflow Automator for Small Businesses

Small businesses often juggle a range of repetitive tasks—responding to customer inquiries, managing inventory, updating spreadsheets, sending invoices, or handling social media posts. Automating these workflows with AI agents can save time, reduce error rates, and boost productivity. This section walks you through building a Workflow Automator using LangGraph and CrewAI that acts as a digital operations manager.

Defining the Use Case

Imagine a small e-commerce shop that wants to automate the daily routine of checking new orders, notifying the packing team, updating inventory, and sending shipping confirmations to customers. All these steps can be orchestrated by agents and flows.

Step 1: Identify and Segment Tasks

We'll break the workflow into the following steps:

1. Check for new orders

2. Notify the warehouse

3. Update the inventory system

4. Email shipping confirmation

Each step becomes a task handled by a specialized agent.

Step 2: Build the Agents with CrewAI

from crewai import Agent, Task, Crew

order_checker = Agent(

  role="Order Checker",

  goal="Retrieve all new orders from the order system",

```python
    backstory="Monitors online shop backend for newly placed
orders",

    verbose=True

)


notifier = Agent(

    role="Warehouse Notifier",

    goal="Send the order details to the packing and shipping team",

    backstory="Coordinates with warehouse staff to fulfill
incoming orders",

    verbose=True

)


inventory_updater = Agent(

    role="Inventory Updater",

    goal="Adjust inventory count based on fulfilled orders",

    backstory="Maintains an accurate inventory ledger",
```

```
    verbose=True

)


emailer = Agent(

    role="Customer Emailer",

    goal="Email shipping confirmation to customer once order is
    dispatched",

    backstory="Handles post-order customer communication",

    verbose=True

)
```

Step 3: Define the Flow

```
order_task = Task(description="Fetch all new orders placed in the
last 24 hours.", agent=order_checker)

notify_task = Task(description="Send the orders to the
warehouse team for fulfillment.", agent=notifier)

update_task = Task(description="Update the inventory count for
each item in the orders.", agent=inventory_updater)
```

```
email_task = Task(description="Send a confirmation email to the
customer with tracking details.", agent=mailer)


crew = Crew(

    agents=[order_checker, notifier, inventory_updater, emailer],

    tasks=[order_task, notify_task, update_task, email_task],

    verbose=True

)


output = crew.kickoff()

print(output)
```

Step 4: Add State Control with LangGraph (Optional)

LangGraph helps if you want to implement conditional logic. For
example, if no orders are found, skip the rest of the tasks:

```
import langgraph
```

```python
@langgraph.node

def check_orders(state):

    if state.get("order_count", 0) == 0:

        return {"next": "end"}

    return {"next": "notify"}
```

Deployment Tips

- Schedule it with Cron or n8n to run every hour or day

- Use FastAPI to expose it as a triggerable endpoint

- Store inventory and order state in Firebase, Supabase, or a local database

Personal Insight

Many small businesses aren't aware they can deploy AI agents without deep technical resources. Automating day-to-day operations with LangGraph + CrewAI has helped several clients I've worked with reduce operational overhead significantly. You don't need full-scale ERP software to get results—a few well-designed agents and a consistent schedule can work wonders.

This Workflow Automator blueprint is easily extendable—add agents for social media updates, accounting exports, or support ticket triage depending on your needs.

Chapter 11: Challenges, Ethics & Security

Building and deploying multi-agent systems isn't just a technical feat—it's also a responsibility. As agents take on more tasks autonomously and operate across a variety of domains, developers must account for privacy, safety, accuracy, and ethical usage. This chapter breaks down the core concerns around data privacy, hallucinations, safety, testing, and responsible usage.

11.1 Data Privacy and Security in Agent Workflows

As agent workflows become more sophisticated, they often touch sensitive data like user documents, authentication tokens, customer records, or third-party credentials. Ensuring privacy and security across every stage of these workflows is crucial to build trust and prevent data breaches.

Understand the Flow of Sensitive Data

Start by mapping out where and how data is accessed, stored, and transmitted within your multi-agent system. Identify:

- Which agents need access to which data

- Where temporary or persistent storage occurs

- External APIs or databases involved

This helps set the foundation for minimizing exposure and enforcing access controls.

Principle of Least Privilege

Design agents with narrowly scoped permissions. For instance, if only the summarization agent needs access to a document's content, there's no need for a coordination agent to see it.

from crewai import Agent

document_summarizer = Agent(

  role="Summarizer",

  goal="Extract insights from provided documents",

  backstory="Has secure access to content blobs but no write permissions",

  tools=[summarize_tool],

```
    verbose=True

)
```

This approach limits accidental exposure and ensures each agent only sees what it needs.

Secure Storage and Communication

Use HTTPS for all external communication and encrypt sensitive fields in transit and at rest. When storing tokens, temporary responses, or memory states:

- Use environment variables instead of hardcoding secrets

- Consider managed secret stores like AWS Secrets Manager, GCP Secret Manager, or HashiCorp Vault

- If using a vector database for memory, ensure it supports encryption and access control

```
import os

os.environ["OPENAI_API_KEY"] = get_secret("openai_key")
```

A helper like get_secret() could pull securely from your secret manager.

Containerization and Isolation

For production deployments, isolate agents and tools within Docker containers or serverless functions. This creates clear execution boundaries and reduces the blast radius in case of compromise.

```
# Base container for a LangGraph agent

FROM python:3.11

WORKDIR /app

COPY . .

RUN pip install -r requirements.txt

CMD ["python", "main.py"]
```

Deploying each agent this way with resource limits adds another layer of protection.

Token and API Hygiene

Rotating API keys, avoiding logs that capture secrets, and implementing retry mechanisms with throttling are essential. For example:

```
import openai

from tenacity import retry, stop_after_attempt


@retry(stop=stop_after_attempt(3))

def query_model(prompt):

    return openai.ChatCompletion.create(...)
```

This pattern prevents runaway retries and helps avoid exposing credentials in error logs.

Logging with Caution

When agents generate logs for debugging or auditing, ensure logs are scrubbed of sensitive content. Use structured logging and redact PII where possible.

```
import logging

logger = logging.getLogger("agent")
```

```
logger.info("Summary generated", extra={"doc_id": doc.id, "user":
"[REDACTED]"})
```

Masking identifiable data in logs protects user privacy and
supports compliance with standards like GDPR.

Personal Insight

In projects where agents process emails or internal reports, I've
seen the benefits of fine-grained access control and temporary
tokens firsthand. Instead of sharing full inboxes or folders, scoped
access to specific items significantly reduced audit risks.

Combined with audit logging, secrets management, and
encrypted message queues, this has allowed agents to function
autonomously while remaining within security guidelines.

11.2 Hallucinations, Bias, and Inaccurate Outputs

One of the most persistent challenges in agent-driven systems is
ensuring that generated responses are accurate, grounded, and free
from misleading or biased content. As agents interact with
dynamic environments, pull data from varied sources, and
collaborate autonomously, they're prone to producing
hallucinations—confident-sounding but incorrect outputs—or
surfacing unintended biases.

What Are Hallucinations?

Hallucinations occur when an agent produces responses that are factually incorrect or unverifiable. These often result from:

- Lack of grounding in real data

- Over-reliance on generative models

- Misinterpretation of instructions or ambiguous prompts

For example, a summarizer agent might invent facts that weren't present in the source material:

summary = llm_agent.run("Summarize this quarterly report")

The generated summary might claim increased profits despite no mention of this in the document.

To minimize hallucinations, validate agent output against structured or verified inputs whenever possible.

Bias in Agent Responses

Bias can manifest in how an agent prioritizes, interprets, or frames information. These biases may be inherited from:

- Training data of underlying LLMs

- Prompt phrasing

- Implicit instructions baked into task flows

Consider a customer service agent:

```
agent = Agent(

  role="Support Specialist",

  goal="Assist customers professionally",

  backstory="Handles queries from all demographics fairly",

  tools=[knowledge_base_tool, faq_tool],

)
```

Even with inclusive prompts, subtle biases might influence how issues are prioritized or how tone shifts between users. Regular testing with varied datasets and user profiles helps identify and mitigate these effects.

Techniques to Mitigate Hallucinations and Bias

1. **Ground Responses in Data**: Whenever possible, use retrieval-augmented generation (RAG) to tether answers to real content.

```
from long chain.chains import RetrievalQA

qa_chain = RetrievalQA(combine_documents_chain=llm_chain,
retriever=vectorstore.as_retriever())
```

2. **Prompt Engineering**: Structure prompts to emphasize factual accuracy and provide examples.

```
prompt = "Answer strictly based on the following text. Do not
add information not present."
```

3. **Post-Processing Validation**: Create guardrails to review or cross-check responses before surfacing them to users.

```
def validate_answer(answer):

  if "possibly" in answer or not answer.endswith("."):

    raise ValueError("Answer may be speculative")
```

4. **Chain-of-Thought Reasoning**: Encourage agents to reason step-by-step. This improves transparency and reduces leaps in logic.

```
cot_prompt = "Let's think step by step before answering."
```

5. **Regular Evaluation**: Include synthetic and real datasets for benchmarking output consistency, accuracy, and neutrality.

Personal Insight

While building a multi-agent research assistant, I noticed hallucinations were often amplified when agents passed partially summarized content between each other. Introducing intermediate validation steps between agents helped improve factual accuracy by nearly 40%. Additionally, requiring agents to cite sources or confidence levels nudged the system toward more cautious, grounded outputs.

11.3 Safety Mechanisms for Autonomy

As AI agents become more autonomous, their ability to operate independently across various tasks and environments also introduces risks. Without built-in safeguards, an agent may take unintended actions, loop indefinitely, misuse tools, or access sensitive data improperly. Designing safety mechanisms is critical to ensure these systems behave predictably, reliably, and within boundaries.

Why Safety Mechanisms Matter

Autonomous agents often interact with APIs, tools, and external data sources. They can generate responses, execute code, or communicate with users—all of which involve real-world consequences. A missing safety check can lead to:

- Costly or irreversible actions (e.g., deleting files, sending incorrect reports)

- Exposure of sensitive data

- Infinite loops or runaway processes

Without safety constraints, autonomy can quickly become liability.

Safety Techniques and Patterns

Tool Access Restrictions Limit access to tools based on agent roles, use-cases, or conditions.

```
if agent.role == "Analyst":

  agent.tools = [report_reader, data_summary]

else:

  agent.tools = [safe_tools_only]
```

1. Define granular permissions to avoid over-empowering agents.

Action Confirmation and Human-in-the-Loop (HITL) Require confirmation for high-impact actions or escalate decisions to humans.

```
if action.requires_confirmation:

  send_to_admin_for_approval(action)
```

2. This is especially useful in customer-facing or administrative roles.

Step and Depth Limits Prevent infinite or recursive behavior by setting limits on how many steps or transitions an agent can take.

```
MAX_STEPS = 10

if agent.step_count > MAX_STEPS:

    raise Exception("Agent exceeded allowed autonomy")
```

3.

Context Window Management Ensure agents aren't operating with outdated, irrelevant, or bloated memory windows. Combine long-term memory with active context filtering.

```
current_context = memory.get_recent(5) +
memory.query_relevant(query)
```

4.

Output Validators and Post-Action Hooks Use functions that validate output or sanitize inputs before they're acted upon.

```
def validate_email_response(text):

    if "refund" in text.lower() and not approved:

        raise Exception("Unauthorized refund communication")
```

5. Hooks also allow developers to log or intercept sensitive actions.

CrewAI and LangGraph Safety Controls

LangGraph enables you to define transitions explicitly, giving you control over when and how agents act. You can gate transitions with custom logic:

```
def should_continue(state):

    return state["confidence"] > 0.8 and state["steps"] < 5
```

CrewAI lets you constrain tasks using roles and expected outputs:

```
Task(

    description="Update client record",

    expected_output="Updated record confirmation",

    tools=[crm_api],

    agent=agent,

    output_guard=validate_crm_change

)
```

Personal Insight

While building a multi-agent delegation system, we had a planner agent accidentally dispatch the same task to multiple doer agents, overwhelming the backend with redundant jobs. We introduced a simple lock system at the task queue level and an intent validator to detect duplicates. That small change improved stability significantly and prevented cross-agent collisions.

11.4 Testing and Validation Strategies

Testing and validation are critical for ensuring that AI agent workflows function correctly, safely, and reliably. Unlike traditional software, AI agents operate in dynamic, data-driven environments, which makes rigorous testing both challenging and essential. A well-tested system can adapt to variability while maintaining robustness and predictability.

Why It Matters

Without structured validation, agents may:

- Misinterpret prompts or tool results

- Generate misleading or incomplete outputs

- Fail silently or crash unexpectedly

- Regress in behavior when updated

Robust testing strategies help catch these issues early, improving agent performance, user trust, and deployment success.

Types of Testing

1. **Unit Testing for Agent Components** Test individual components—tools, memory handlers, validators—like any software module.

```
from myagent.tools import summarize_tool


def test_summarize_tool():

    result = summarize_tool("LangGraph allows node control")

    assert "LangGraph" in result
```

2. **Agent Behavior Tests** Simulate prompts and inputs to check how agents respond under different scenarios.

```python
def test_agent_behavior():

    user_input = "Summarize this document: ..."

    result = agent.run(input=user_input)

    assert "summary" in result.lower()
```

3. **End-to-End (E2E) Workflow Tests** Validate full
   workflows including memory access, tool execution, and
   output generation.

```python
def test_full_workflow():

    state = graph.run({"query": "Get revenue trends"})

    assert state["final_output"] is not None
```

Use mock tools or test stubs for expensive API calls to improve
repeatability.

4. **Edge Case Handling** Design tests for
   out-of-distribution prompts, invalid inputs, or missing
   context.

```
def test_missing_input():

    try:

        agent.run(input=None)

    except ValueError as e:

        assert "missing" in str(e)
```

5. **Regression Testing** Track behavior over time as models, tools, or configurations change. Store test cases and snapshots of outputs to detect unintended shifts.

Validation Techniques

- **Output Assertions**: Check that outputs conform to expected formats or schemas.

- **Confidence Thresholds**: Ensure agents act only when their certainty exceeds a safe limit.

- **Human-in-the-Loop Review**: Manually audit random samples or edge-case results.

- **Red Teaming**: Proactively stress test workflows with adversarial prompts.

Continuous Testing Pipelines

In production environments, integrate tests into CI/CD pipelines. Use tools like pytest, unittest, or LangSmith for automated trace-based testing:

pytest tests/

LangGraph and CrewAI support trace logging, making it easier to rerun and analyze specific decision paths.

Personal Insight

When working on an AI customer support bot, we encountered issues where the agent would answer policy questions with hallucinated terms. We introduced a simple validation pipeline: answers were checked against a keyword whitelist, and any deviation was flagged for review. That dramatically reduced false responses and boosted our QA confidence.

11.5 Responsible Use of AI Agents

Creating AI agents isn't just about engineering—it's about making ethical decisions that shape the way users experience and trust these systems. As developers and architects, we hold responsibility for ensuring that the agents we build are transparent, fair, and beneficial to users and stakeholders.

Why Responsibility Matters

AI agents can operate autonomously, scale decisions, and influence real-world outcomes. Without responsible design and governance, they can:

- Spread misinformation

- Reinforce harmful biases

- Invade user privacy

- Disempower human oversight

Responsible use ensures your system doesn't just work, but works *for good*—in ways that align with ethical principles, business values, and regulatory expectations.

Core Principles for Responsible AI Agents

1. **Transparency** Ensure agents can explain their actions
    and decisions in a human-understandable way.

```
response, reasoning = agent.run_with_explanation("Why was my
refund denied?")

print("Decision rationale:", reasoning)
```

Avoid black-box behavior. Annotate actions, expose tool calls, and
summarize memory usage where possible.

2. **User Consent and Privacy** Respect data boundaries.
    Prompt for permissions before accessing or storing
    personal information. Mask sensitive details from logs or
    persistent memory.

```
if not user.has_consented("store_email"):

    raise PermissionError("Consent required for storing email")
```

Use environment variables or secret managers for all tokens and
personal data references.

3. **Bias Mitigation** Audit prompts, training data, and responses for biased language or outcomes. Tools like Fairlearn, AI Fairness 360, and embedding comparison methods can help identify problematic behavior.

```python
from sklearn.metrics import demographic_parity_difference

score = demographic_parity_difference(y_true, y_pred,
sensitive_features=sensitive_col)
```

Retrain agents, revise examples, or apply filters to enforce neutrality where necessary.

4. **Bounded Autonomy** Clearly defines what an agent can and cannot do. Use hard-coded rules, token thresholds, or tool restrictions to constrain risky behaviors.

```python
allowed_tools = ["search_tool", "summarizer"]

agent.configure(tools=allowed_tools)
```

Avoid giving agents decision-making authority over sensitive or irreversible outcomes without human review.

5. **Human Oversight** Incorporate human-in-the-loop controls, especially for high-risk decisions. This can mean:

- Routing sensitive outputs to a human reviewer

- Logging all actions for audit trails

- Letting users override agent behavior

Implementation Example: Ethical Guardrails

Here's a minimal example of enforcing content and context constraints before the agent replies:

```
banned_topics = ["violence", "medical advice"]
```

```
def ethical_guardrails(prompt):

    for topic in banned_topics:

        if topic in prompt.lower():

            return "I'm not allowed to discuss that topic."

    return agent.run(prompt)
```

This kind of filtering can be enhanced with NLP classifiers or embeddings for context-aware safety checks.

Evolving with Governance

As regulation matures (e.g., EU AI Act, U.S. executive orders), compliance isn't optional. Be proactive:

- Document your design choices

- Maintain logs of training data, prompts, and outputs

- Build explainability and auditability from day one

Personal Insight

When deploying a workflow automation agent for finance clients, we initially allowed it to summarize and route any document. During beta testing, it misrouted a sensitive contract because it misread a filename. We implemented a policy where contracts required checksum verification and multi-step human approval. This slowed things down—but made it safer and restored client trust.

Chapter 12: The Future of Multi-Agent AI Systems

The evolution of AI agents is accelerating rapidly, and multi-agent systems (MAS) are taking center stage in the design of scalable, adaptive, and intelligent software. While earlier chapters have focused on building, deploying, and maintaining agent workflows, this chapter looks ahead—exploring where the field is heading and how developers, researchers, and businesses can position themselves for success.

12.1 Trends in Autonomous AI

Autonomous AI is maturing rapidly and becoming indispensable in business, research, and consumer applications. This section explores the most impactful trends shaping the way we design and deploy intelligent agents today—and what to expect tomorrow.

1. Agent Swarms and Decentralized Collaboration

Inspired by nature—like how ants forage or birds flock—agent swarms use decentralized coordination. Instead of relying on a single orchestrator, they collaborate through signals, goals, or shared states. These swarms are being used in:

- Disaster response simulations

- Distributed sensor analysis

- Real-time gaming AI

- Traffic routing and logistics

In practice, building agent swarms involves defining simple local rules and leveraging a shared memory layer or message queue. Here's a minimal example using LangGraph with Redis for agent coordination:

```python
# Define a shared Redis-backed memory

from langgraph.graph import StateGraph

from crewai import Crew, Agent

import redis


redis_client = redis.Redis()


def shared_state(key):
```

```
return redis_client.get(key)


def update_state(key, value):

    redis_client.set(key, value)



# Each agent modifies the shared state based on its role
```

2. Cloud-Native and Serverless Agents

Frameworks like LangGraph and CrewAI are embracing serverless and cloud-native designs. This allows:

- Scalable execution with managed compute

- Pay-per-inference cost models

- Integration with CI/CD workflows

For example, deploying a LangGraph pipeline using AWS Lambda or Google Cloud Functions ensures low-cost and elastic resource usage. Developers only need to package workflows with FastAPI, expose them via HTTP, and use API Gateway to trigger them.

3. Tool-Augmented Reasoning

Agents no longer operate in isolation. They are now expected to:

- Pull data from APIs

- Query vector stores or databases

- Read documents and spreadsheets

Instead of producing answers through language generation alone, modern agents synthesize tool outputs. CrewAI's tool abstraction lets you build agents that reason over structured responses:

from crewai_tools import SerpApiTool, CsvReaderTool

agent = Agent(

  name="Market Analyst",

  tools=[SerpApiTool(), CsvReaderTool()],

  goal="Find current competitors and analyze pricing from the latest spreadsheet"

)

4. Real-Time, Low-Latency Execution

With agents taking over responsibilities like customer support, monitoring, or trading, latency matters. Agents must be able to:

- Process requests in milliseconds

- Stream responses when possible

- Use caching or pre-fetching techniques

FastAPI or LangChain's streaming tools make this easier. Combined with Redis or memory stores like Qdrant, developers can implement near-instantaneous lookups and workflows.

5. Hybrid Architectures: Symbolic + Neural + Heuristics

Relying solely on LLMs for decision-making is often brittle. New agent designs are blending:

- Symbolic planners (e.g., decision trees)

- Neural inference (e.g., GPT-4)

- Rule-based logic (e.g., if-then constraints)

This balance ensures higher reliability, especially in high-stakes workflows like legal compliance, autonomous vehicles, or finance.

LangGraph's graph control allows this hybrid logic to be expressed in custom state transitions and validation checkpoints.

12.2 Multi-Modal and Embodied Agents

AI agents are no longer confined to text inputs and outputs. The future of multi-agent systems is increasingly multi-modal—meaning agents that understand and interact through images, audio, video, and sensor data. When these agents are embedded in physical or virtual environments, they become **embodied agents**, capable of perceiving and acting in the world.

This section explores how these advancements are changing agent design, with practical examples you can build upon.

Understanding Multi-Modality in Agents
Multi-modal agents can process and respond using multiple input/output types, such as:

- Text + Images (e.g., image captioning or visual question answering)

- Audio + Text (e.g., voice assistants that listen and speak)

- Video + Language (e.g., analyzing surveillance footage with descriptions)

- Sensor data + Actuation (e.g., robotic arms or drones)

Thanks to models like OpenAI's GPT-4 with Vision, Google's Gemini, and open frameworks like LLaVA or CLIP, multi-modal capabilities are now accessible through APIs and OSS tooling.

Example: Image-Based Document Analysis Agent
Let's build a simple document-reading assistant using OpenAI's GPT-4 Vision capabilities and LangGraph:

```
from openai import OpenAI

from PIL import Image


client = OpenAI()


image_path = "receipt.jpg"

image_data = Image.open(image_path)
```

```
response = client.chat.completions.create(

  model="gpt-4-vision-preview",

  messages=[

   {"role": "user", "content": [

     {"type": "text", "text": "Extract total amount from this
receipt."},

     {"type": "image_url", "image_url": {"url":
"data:image/jpeg;base64,..."}}

   ]}

  ],

  max_tokens=300

)



print(response.choices[0].message.content)
```

This type of agent is invaluable for automating tasks like invoice
parsing, identity verification, and compliance reviews.

Embodied Agents in Action

Embodied agents are typically integrated into virtual environments (like simulators) or physical platforms (like robots or IoT devices). They can:

- Navigate physical space using computer vision and depth sensors

- Manipulate objects with actuators

- React to stimuli in real-time (e.g., temperature, pressure, audio)

Tools like **Unity ML-Agents, Habitat AI**, and **NVIDIA Isaac** allow simulation-based training. Meanwhile, frameworks like **ROS (Robot Operating System)** connect agents to real-world sensors and motors.

Practical Example: Simulated Cleaning Bot Agent with Unity + LangChain

While a full robotics setup is outside the scope here, you can simulate an embodied agent in Unity that:

1. Observes a room

2. Decides the next cleaning step using LangChain

3. Sends commands to Unity's environment engine

```
from langchain.agents import initialize_agent, Tool
from long chain.lmms import OpenAI


llm = OpenAI()


tools = [
    Tool(
        name="MoveTo",
        func=lambda loc: f"Moving to {loc}",
        description="Navigate to a specific location"
    ),
    Tool(
        name="PickUpItem",
        func=lambda item: f"Picking up {item}",
```

```
        description="Pick up an item from the ground"

    )

]



agent = initialize_agent(tools, llm,
agent="zero-shot-react-description", verbose=True)



task = "Clean the spilled coffee in the kitchen"

agent.run(task)
```

Real-World Use Cases

- **Retail**: Shelf-monitoring bots detect empty shelves or misplaced items

- **Healthcare**: Multi-modal agents interpret X-rays, CT scans, and patient notes

- **Security**: Surveillance bots use video + thermal imaging to flag anomalies

- **Education**: Virtual tutors that interpret drawings, spoken questions, and gestures

Design Challenges and Considerations

Multi-modal and embodied agents introduce new complexities:

- **Latency**: Processing image or video inputs adds computational delay

- **Alignment**: Output behavior must align with user goals across modalities

- **Safety**: Especially for embodied agents, real-world actions can have physical consequences

To mitigate risk, always start with simulation environments or "dry runs" before deploying agents to real-world systems..

12.3 Self-Evolving and Self-Healing Systems

One of the most powerful directions for multi-agent AI is the emergence of systems that can **evolve their own capabilities** and **recover from failures autonomously**. These traits are critical for building resilient applications that need to run long-term with minimal human oversight.

Self-evolving and self-healing systems mimic biological processes like adaptation and regeneration. With the right design, agents can:

- Improve their own performance through feedback

- Update tool sets or knowledge bases dynamically

- Detect, isolate, and resolve errors without manual intervention

Let's break down how this is done in practice.

What Makes an Agent System 'Self-Evolving'?
A self-evolving system includes components that can adjust their own behavior or structure based on:

- Performance metrics

- User feedback

- Environmental changes

- API/tool usage patterns

For example, an AI agent that retrieves answers from documents could monitor which responses are consistently marked as unhelpful, then re-tune its retrieval parameters or swap in a different vector store.

A Minimal Self-Improving Agent Loop

```
import json

from langchain.agents import initialize_agent, Tool

from long chain.lmms import OpenAI


llm = OpenAI()


feedback_log = []


def store_feedback(input_text, result, user_rating):
    feedback_log.append({
        "input": input_text,
        "result": result,
```

```python
        "rating": user_rating

    })


def adjust_strategy():

    low_scores = [f for f in feedback_log if f["rating"] < 3]

    if len(low_scores) > 5:

        print("Updating prompt template or switching tool due to
poor feedback...")


agent = initialize_agent(tools=[], llm=llm,
agent="zero-shot-react-description")


# Simulated loop

input_text = "Find recent financial news about Tesla"

result = agent.run(input_text)


# Simulate user rating it 2/5
```

```
store_feedback(input_text, result, user_rating=2)
```

```
adjust_strategy()
```

This is a toy example, but it captures the feedback → analysis → improvement loop.

Self-Healing: Recovery from Failures

Self-healing focuses on resilience. It allows agents to detect:

- Crashes or timeouts

- Failed tool/API calls

- Invalid outputs or infinite loops

Then, instead of halting, the system:

- Re-tries with backup logic

- Switches to alternative tools

- Logs and reports but continues operating

Basic Retry Logic in LangChain Tools

from langchain.tools import Tool

import requests

def fetch_api_data():

    try:

        res = requests.get("https://some-api.com/data", timeout=5)

        res.raise_for_status()

        return res.json()

    except Exception as e:

        return f"Primary API failed: {e}. Attempting fallback..."

def fallback():

    return {"data": "This is fallback data."}

```
fetch_data_tool = Tool(

    name="FetchData",

    func=lambda _: fetch_api_data() or fallback(),

    description="Grabs live data with retry logic"

)
```

Techniques That Enable Evolution & Healing

- **Agent Memory:** Store past actions and results (LangGraph makes this easy)

- **Dynamic Tool Management:** Agents swap or update tools at runtime

- **Introspective Loops:** Agents analyze their own outputs and adjust

- **Behavior Trees or State Machines:** These allow adaptive planning logic

- **Health Monitoring:** Custom checks (e.g., latency, API errors, system state)

Advanced Tip: Build a Monitoring Agent Inside the System

Create a watchdog agent that:

- Observes logs

- Detects anomalies

- Triggers restarts or fallback logic

```
def monitor_logs(logs):

    for log in logs:

        if "error" in log.lower():

            print("Anomaly detected. Initiating recovery protocol.")
```

Real-World Examples

- **AutoML systems** tune their own model pipelines based on training results

- **Customer support agents** evolve by incorporating feedback and adjusting flows

- **RPA bots** heal from DOM changes or API version updates

Key Considerations

- You must **log everything**. Visibility is the first step toward self-healing.

- Too much autonomy without constraints can lead to instability. Use guardrails.

- Testing in sandboxed environments is essential before allowing self-evolving logic in production.

Self-evolving and self-healing systems mark a shift from static automation to adaptive intelligence. With careful design, these agents not only get smarter over time—they become more trustworthy and efficient.

12.4 Emerging Frameworks and Open Source Projects

The rise of multi-agent systems has sparked an explosion of innovation in open-source frameworks that make it easier to build intelligent agents capable of collaborating, reasoning, and acting autonomously. These tools aren't just abstract platforms—they're enabling developers, researchers, and startups to deploy powerful systems that were nearly impossible to build just a few years ago.

Below is a focused overview of the most relevant frameworks today, what makes each of them special, and how to integrate them into your own agent workflows.

LangGraph: Declarative Graph-Based Agent Flows

LangGraph extends LangChain to support graph-based execution models for agents. Instead of writing imperative logic, you define nodes (agents or tools) and edges (control flow). This structure is ideal for complex multi-agent workflows where each node passes state to the next based on outcomes.

Use when:

- You need fine-grained control over agent interaction and memory

- Your application involves conditional routing, retries, or branching

- You're building workflows where visibility and debuggability matter

Step-by-Step Example

from langgraph.graph import StateGraph, END

```python
# Simple node that transforms text
def capitalize_node(state):
    return {"output": state["input"].upper()}


graph = StateGraph()

graph.add_node("capitalize", capitalize_node)

graph.set_entry_point("capitalize")

graph.add_edge("capitalize", END)


app = graph.compile()

result = app.invoke({"input": "langgraph rocks"})
```

```
print(result)  # {'output': 'LANGGRAPH ROCKS'}
```

LangGraph makes your multi-agent system predictable, modular, and easy to test.

CrewAI: Role-Based Teams with Delegation

CrewAI models agent systems like collaborative teams. Each agent has a role, goal, and tools. Tasks are assigned to agents, which then communicate and delegate intelligently. The structure mimics human workflows—perfect for real-world use cases like research, writing, or planning.

Use when:

- You need autonomous coordination between specialist agents

- You're designing pipelines like "research → write → review"

- You want natural-language, goal-driven execution

Basic Setup

```python
from crewai import Agent, Task, Crew


# Define agents

researcher = Agent(name="Researcher", role="Find relevant data")

writer = Agent(name="Writer", role="Compose summaries")


# Assign tasks

task1 = Task(description="Research use cases of AI in healthcare", agent=researcher)

task2 = Task(description="Write a report based on findings", agent=writer)


# Build the crew

crew = Crew(agents=[researcher, writer], tasks=[task1, task2])

crew.kickoff()
```

CrewAI is great for higher-level orchestration where agents act like team members.

AutoGen: Conversational Agent Orchestration

Developed by Microsoft, AutoGen is designed for multi-agent systems that communicate in a conversational format. Each agent can act, reason, and interact through structured messaging. It's especially useful for research, experimentation, and building "chat-between-agents" setups.

Use when:

- You want agents to collaborate via dialogue

- You need centralized memory and context between steps

- You're building systems that simulate human conversation or negotiation

Example

from autogen import AssistantAgent, UserProxyAgent

assistant = AssistantAgent(name="Assistant")

```
reviewer = AssistantAgent(name="Reviewer")

user = UserProxyAgent(name="User")



# Kick off conversation

user.initiate_chat(assistant, message="Summarize the article on
climate change.")

assistant.initiate_chat(reviewer)
```

AutoGen's conversational model is highly intuitive for chaining
multiple reasoning agents.

AgentVerse: Simulated Environments for Agents

AgentVerse enables multi-agent simulations in virtual
environments. It's tailored for use cases like urban planning,
autonomous behavior testing, or social simulations. The
framework supports interaction rules, time progression, and
spatial awareness.

Use when:

- You're building spatial or social simulations

- You want to study emergent behavior or policy effects

- Your agents need a persistent environment to operate in

AgentVerse is experimental but powerful for systems requiring an environment-like context.

MetaGPT: SOP-Driven Software Development Teams

MetaGPT takes agent collaboration a step further by implementing Standard Operating Procedures (SOPs). Each agent plays a professional role—product manager, engineer, QA, etc.—and follows defined behavior templates. It's optimized for structured software tasks.

Use when:

- You want a team of agents to build apps or generate code

- You need consistency across projects or iterations

- Your workflow benefits from defined stages like spec, design, build

While more rigid, MetaGPT is ideal for automating project pipelines with predictable outputs.

How to Choose

Here's a quick decision chart:

Scenario	Framework
Custom workflows with state & logic	LangGraph
Role-based collaboration	CrewAI
Agent-to-agent conversation	AutoGen
Simulation of behaviors or policies	AgentVerse
Software team automation	MetaGPT

If you're experimenting, try CrewAI or LangGraph for flexibility. For large-scale simulation or product pipelines, consider AgentVerse or MetaGPT.

Best Practices for Working with Open Source Tools

1. **Read the source code** – It's the best way to understand how agents are coordinated and how memory is shared.

2. **Contribute early** – Open source projects evolve fast. Reporting bugs or suggesting features helps the whole community.

3. **Build wrappers** – Abstract away tool-specific quirks so you can swap frameworks if needed later.

4. **Test workflows continuously** – Multi-agent systems are prone to logic drift and brittle integrations.

12.5 Building a Career or Business Around AI Agents

If you've been hands-on with multi-agent systems through this book, you already have the foundations to turn this into something bigger—either as a career path or a business opportunity. The industry is rapidly evolving, but there's already demand for developers, consultants, and entrepreneurs who know how to architect intelligent, collaborative agents. Whether you're looking to freelance, join a company, or build your own SaaS product, this guide breaks down how to position yourself for success.

Understand the Opportunity Landscape

Multi-agent systems aren't just a technical curiosity—they're at the heart of several high-growth fields:

- **Enterprise automation**: Think automated report generation, compliance workflows, and knowledge assistants.

- **Developer productivity**: Multi-agent tools that generate, test, and debug code collaboratively.

- **AI customer support**: Autonomous agents that resolve tickets, escalate issues, and personalize experiences.

- **Research & writing**: Agents that explore academic databases, summarize findings, and generate reports.

Each of these verticals has both B2B and B2C opportunities. As adoption increases, companies will need professionals who can prototype, deploy, and maintain agent-powered systems.

Paths to Get Involved

There are three primary tracks for monetizing your skillset:

1. **Freelancing / Consulting**

    o   Offer services on Upwork, Toptal, or AI-specific networks (like Latent Space or LangChain Experts).

    o   Focus on specific deliverables like "Build a LangGraph agent workflow" or "Automate a business process with CrewAI."

2. **Product Development**

    o   Build a SaaS product powered by agents.

    o   Examples: AI resume optimizers, market research bots, autonomous email sorters.

3. **Career Roles**

    o   Positions like "AI Workflow Engineer" or "LLM Application Developer" are becoming more common.

- Employers look for experience with LangChain, vector databases, agent orchestration, and prompt engineering.

Building a Portfolio That Gets You Hired

Instead of just listing skills, demonstrate impact through mini-projects. Here are examples that can double as both portfolio items and GitHub repos:

- **AI Research Assistant with LangGraph**: Show how agents coordinate to summarize research papers.

- **Customer Support Crew with CrewAI**: Demonstrate role-based delegation for resolving support tickets.

- **Real Estate Deal Analyzer**: Build an agent that scrapes listings, filters by investment logic, and summarizes opportunities.

Pro Tip: Add a README with a clear explanation, a diagram of the agent workflow, and a Loom video walkthrough. Most recruiters won't run your code, but they will read and watch.

Monetizing with Minimal Overhead

If you lean entrepreneurial, here's how to build low-cost agent-based products:

1. **Identify a niche pain point**
   Talk to professionals in domains like HR, finance, or law. Ask: "What do you spend too much time on that a smart assistant could handle?"

2. **Build a simple prototype**
   Use Streamlit or FastAPI to deploy. LangGraph or CrewAI to orchestrate.

3. **Charge for access**
   Start small: $10/mo for a productivity bot that drafts real estate summaries. Iterate with user feedback.

Example: Simple SaaS Bot

```
app/
├── main.py      # FastAPI app
├── agents.py    # CrewAI logic
├── templates/
│   └── email.jinja
```

main.py

```python
from fastapi import FastAPI, Request

from agents import run_agent_workflow


app = FastAPI()


@app.post("/generate")
async def generate_summary(request: Request):
    data = await request.json()

    return run_agent_workflow(data["query"])
```

agents.py

```python
from crewai import Agent, Task, Crew


def run_agent_workflow(query):
```

```
agent = Agent(name="Summarizer", role="Extract insights")

task = Task(description=f"Summarize: {query}", agent=agent)

crew = Crew(agents=[agent], tasks=[task])

return {"summary": crew.kickoff()}
```

Deploy this to Render or Railway, and you've got a working micro-product.

Networking and Visibility

To get traction in the AI agents space, consider:

- **Open Source Contributions**
  Contribute to LangGraph, CrewAI, or similar tools. Even documentation PRs go a long way.

- **X/Twitter Threads**
  Share architecture diagrams, lessons learned, and code snippets. The AI dev community is very active and collaborative.

- **Online Courses or Workshops**
  Host a tutorial on Gumroad, or launch a cohort-based course. People are willing to pay for guided, real-world

insights.

Sustainable Differentiation

Multi-agent AI is still early. You can stand out by focusing on:

- **Reliability and Evaluation**: Build systems that don't just run, but are measurable and testable.

- **Vertical Expertise**: Be the "agent person" in a specific industry (healthcare, education, etc.)

- **Responsible Design**: Incorporate transparency, safety nets, and fallback strategies—these are huge selling points in enterprise settings.

Conclusion

You've just completed a deep dive into one of the most transformative paradigms in AI: multi-agent systems. What started with understanding basic agents and workflows has now evolved into a practical framework for building intelligent, scalable, and autonomous applications that can reason, collaborate, and act with minimal human intervention. You've seen how LangGraph and CrewAI serve as the backbone for this transformation—equipping you to turn abstract AI goals into deployed, functioning systems.

But this book was never just about tools. It's about thinking in systems, designing for autonomy, and engineering trust into intelligent workflows. It's about asking better questions, framing the right tasks, and building agents that can not only act but improve over time. These are the skills that will set you apart as the AI landscape matures.

A few final takeaways to carry with you:

- **Start simple, evolve fast**: Your first agent doesn't need to be perfect. Focus on getting something working end-to-end, then iterate.

- **Measure what matters**: Test for reliability, monitor for drift, and evaluate performance regularly. An agent that works today may behave differently tomorrow.

- **Human-in-the-loop isn't a crutch—it's a feature**: Use humans to guide, audit, and evolve your agent workflows. The goal isn't full autonomy; it's intelligent delegation.

- **Don't build alone**: The open-source agent ecosystem is growing rapidly. Engage with the community, share your builds, ask for feedback, and collaborate.

Personally, I've found working with agent-based systems to be more than just technically rewarding—it's a shift in mindset. It forces you to think not just like a developer, but like a system architect, an orchestrator, and occasionally, a philosopher of human-machine interaction. The lessons you've learned here will apply far beyond this domain: to automation, software design, even organizational structure.

So what's next? Build something real. Solve a niche problem. Contribute to a framework. Or launch a product powered by agents. The field is wide open for builders who can bridge technical depth with practical application.

You now have the knowledge, the tools, and—most importantly—the perspective. Go build the future of intelligent systems. One agent at a time.

www.ingramcontent.com/pod-product-compliance
Lightning Source LLC
LaVergne TN
LVHW022332060326
832902LV00022B/4005